Microsoft®
EXCEL 97

— SIMPLIFIED —

IN FULL COLOR

VISUAL **3D** SERIES

by: maranGraphics' D

D1501801

Corporate Sales

Contact maranGraphics
Phone: (905) 890-3300
(800) 469-6616
Fax: (905) 890-9434

Canadian Trade Sales

Contact Prentice Hall Canada
Phone: (416) 293-3621
(800) 567-3800
Fax: (416) 299-2529

Visit our Web site at:
http://www.maran.com

Microsoft® Excel 97 Simplified

Copyright©   1996, 1997 by maranGraphics Inc.
                5755 Coopers Avenue
                Mississauga, Ontario, Canada
                L4Z 1R9

Screen shots reprinted by permission from Microsoft Corporation.

Canadian Cataloguing in Publication Data

Maran, Ruth, 1970-
    Excel 97 simplified

(Visual 3-D series)
Written by Ruth Maran.
Includes index.
ISBN 1-896283-29-2

1. Microsoft Excel for Windows (Computer file) .
2. Business - Computer programs.   3. Electronic spreadsheets
- Computer programs.   I. maranGraphics' Development Group.
II. Title.   III. Series.

HF5548.4.M523M366 1997   005.369   C97-930437-7

Printed in the United States of America

10   9   8   7   6   5   4   3   2   1

Trademark Acknowledgments

maranGraphics Inc. has attempted to include trademark information
for products, services and companies referred to in this guide.
Although maranGraphics Inc. has made reasonable efforts in
gathering this information, it cannot guarantee its accuracy.

All other brand names and product names used in this book
are trademarks, registered trademarks, or trade names of their
respective holders. maranGraphics Inc. is not associated with any
product or vendor mentioned in this book.

**FOR PURPOSES OF ILLUSTRATING THE CONCEPTS AND
TECHNIQUES DESCRIBED IN THIS BOOK, THE AUTHOR HAS
CREATED VARIOUS NAMES, COMPANY NAMES, MAILING
ADDRESSES, E-MAIL ADDRESSES AND PHONE NUMBERS,
ALL OF WHICH ARE FICTITIOUS. ANY RESEMBLANCE OF
THESE FICTITIOUS NAMES, COMPANY NAMES, MAILING
ADDRESSES, E-MAIL ADDRESSES AND PHONE NUMBERS TO
ANY ACTUAL PERSON, COMPANY AND/OR ORGANIZATION IS
UNINTENTIONAL AND PURELY COINCIDENTAL.**

©1996, 1997
maranGraphics, Inc.

The animated characters are the
copyright of maranGraphics, Inc.

Microsoft® EXCEL 97

— SIMPLIFIED —

IN FULL COLOR

VISUAL **3D** SERIES

maranGraphics™

*Every maranGraphics book represents
the extraordinary vision and commitment of a unique family:
the Maran family of Toronto, Canada.*

Back Row (from left to right): *Sherry Maran, Rob Maran, Richard Maran, Maxine Maran, Jill Maran.*
Front Row (from left to right): *Judy Maran, Ruth Maran.*

Richard Maran is the company founder and its inspirational leader. He developed maranGraphics' proprietary communication technology called "visual grammar." This book is built on that technology—empowering readers with the easiest and quickest way to learn about computers.

Ruth Maran is the Author and Architect—a role Richard established that now bears Ruth's distinctive touch. She creates the words and visual structure that are the basis for the books.

Judy Maran is the Project Coordinator. She works with Ruth, Richard and the highly talented maranGraphics illustrators, designers and editors to transform Ruth's material into its final form.

Rob Maran is the Technical and Production Specialist. He makes sure the state-of-the-art technology used to create these books always performs as it should.

Sherry Maran manages the Reception, Order Desk and any number of areas that require immediate attention and a helping hand.

Jill Maran is a jack-of-all-trades and dynamo who fills in anywhere she's needed anytime she's back from university.

Maxine Maran is the Business Manager and family sage. She maintains order in the business and family—and keeps everything running smoothly.

Oh, and three other family members are seated on the sofa. These graphic disk characters help make it fun and easy to learn about computers. They're part of the extended maranGraphics family.

Credits

Author & Architect:
Ruth Maran

**Copy Development
& Screen Captures:**
Brad Hilderley
Alison MacAlpine

Project Coordinator:
Judy Maran

Proofreaders:
Wanda Lawrie
Peter Lejcar
Tina Veltri
Carol Barclay

Layout Designers:
Christie Van Duin
Tamara Poliquin

Illustrations & Screens:
Chris K.C. Leung
Russell Marini
Ben Lee
Jeff Jones

Indexer:
Kelleigh Wing

Post Production:
Robert Maran

Acknowledgments

Thanks to the dedicated staff of maranGraphics, including Carol
Barclay, Jamie Bell, Francisco Ferreira, Brad Hilderley, Jeff Jones,
Wanda Lawrie, Ben Lee, Peter Lejcar, Chris K.C. Leung, Alison
MacAlpine, Michael W. MacDonald, Jill Maran, Judy Maran, Maxine
Maran, Robert Maran, Sherry Maran, Russ Marini, Tamara Poliquin,
Christie Van Duin, Tina Veltri, Paul Whitehead and Kelleigh Wing.

Finally, to Richard Maran who originated the easy-to-use graphic
format of this guide. Thank you for your inspiration and guidance.

TABLE OF CONTENTS

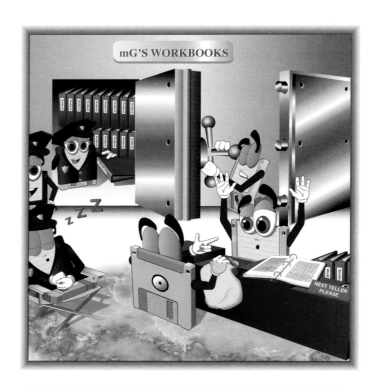

CHAPTER 3

Edit Your Worksheets

CHAPTER 4

Work with Formulas and Functions

TABLE OF CONTENTS

CHAPTER 5

Change Your Screen Display

CHAPTER 6

Format Your Worksheets

CHAPTER 7

Print Your Worksheets

TABLE OF CONTENTS

CHAPTER 12

Excel and the Internet

CHAPTER 11

Manage Data in a List

CHAPTER 1

GETTING STARTED

Are you ready to begin using Microsoft Excel 97? This chapter will help you get started.

CLICK
CLICK

Digital Camera

INTRODUCTION

Excel helps you organize, analyze and attractively present data.

Editing
Excel lets you efficiently enter and edit data in your worksheets.

Formatting
There are many features in Excel that help you enhance the appearance of your worksheets.

Formulas and Functions
Excel provides powerful tools to calculate and analyze data in your worksheets.

Charts

Excel helps you create colorful charts from your worksheet data.

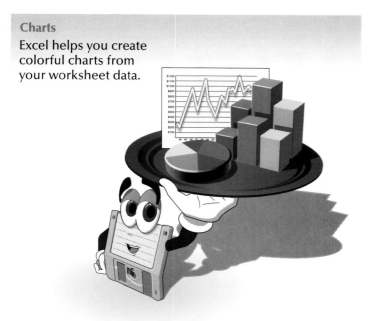

Graphics

Excel comes with many types of graphics that you can use to enhance the appearance of your worksheets and charts.

Managing Data in a List

Excel provides powerful tools that allow you to easily manage and analyze a large collection of information.

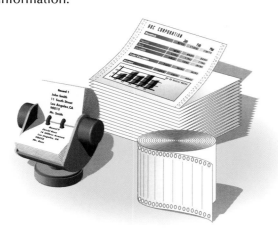

The Internet

Excel offers features that help you take advantage of the Internet. You can make worksheets you create available on your company's intranet or the Web.

USING THE MOUSE

A mouse is a hand-held device that lets you select and move items on your screen.

Holding the Mouse

Resting your hand on the mouse, use your thumb and two rightmost fingers to move the mouse on your desk. Use your two remaining fingers to press the mouse buttons.

Moving the Mouse

When you move the mouse on your desk, the mouse pointer on your screen moves in the same direction.

The mouse pointer assumes different shapes (examples: ✛, I or ↖), depending on its location on your screen and the task you are performing.

Cleaning the Mouse

A ball under the mouse senses movement. You should occasionally remove and clean this ball to ensure smooth motion of the mouse.

MOUSE ACTIONS

Click
Press and release the left mouse button.

Double-Click
Quickly press and release the left mouse button twice.

Drag and Drop
Move the mouse pointer ( ) over an object on your screen and then press and hold down the left mouse button. Still holding down the mouse button, move the mouse to where you want to place the object and then release the mouse button.

MICROSOFT INTELLIMOUSE

The new Microsoft IntelliMouse has a wheel between the left and right mouse buttons. Moving this wheel lets you quickly scroll through information on your screen.

You can also zoom in or out with the Microsoft IntelliMouse by holding down Ctrl on your keyboard as you move the wheel.

When you start Excel, a blank worksheet appears. You can enter data into this worksheet.

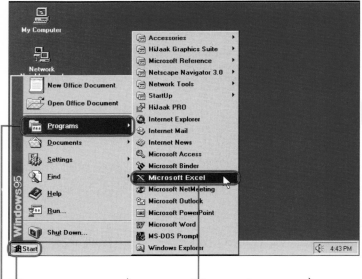

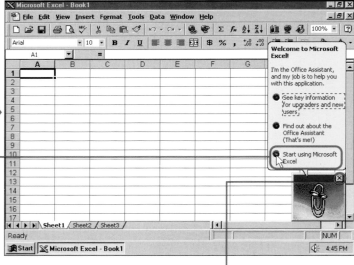

1 Move the mouse ⊳ over **Start** and then press the left mouse button.

2 Move the mouse ⊳ over **Programs**.

3 Move the mouse ⊳ over **Microsoft Excel** and then press the left mouse button.

■ The **Microsoft Excel** window appears, displaying a blank worksheet.

■ If you are starting Excel for the first time, the Office Assistant welcome appears.

4 To start using Excel, move the mouse ⊳ over this option and then press the left mouse button.

■ To hide the Office Assistant, move the mouse ⊳ over ☒ and then press the left mouse button.

Note: For more information on the Office Assistant, refer to page 20.

8

THE EXCEL SCREEN

The Excel screen displays several items to help you perform tasks efficiently.

Menu Bar
Contains commands that let you perform tasks.

Toolbars
Contain buttons to help you quickly select common commands.

Formula Bar
Displays the cell reference and contents of the active cell.

Status Bar
Displays information about the task you are performing.

Worksheet Tabs
An Excel file is called a workbook. Each workbook is divided into several worksheets. Excel displays a tab for each worksheet.

A workbook is similar to a three-ring binder that contains several sheets of paper.

WORKSHEET BASICS

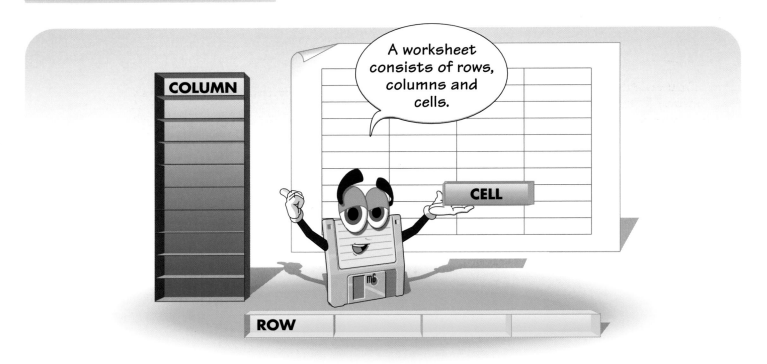

ROWS, COLUMNS AND CELLS

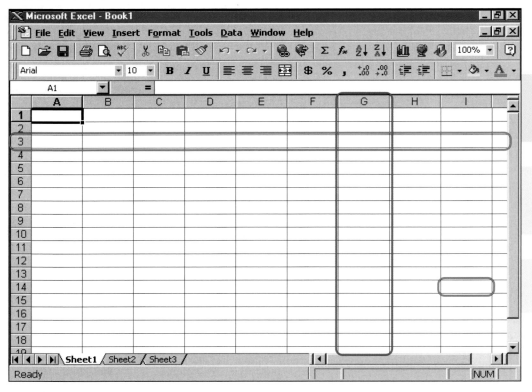

Row

A horizontal line of boxes. A number identifies each row.

Column

A vertical line of boxes. A letter identifies each column.

Cell

One box in a worksheet.

10

You enter information into the active cell in your worksheet.

THE ACTIVE CELL

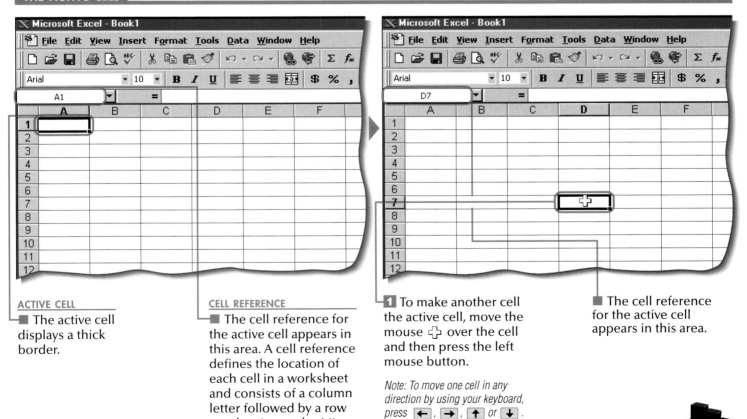

ACTIVE CELL

■ The active cell displays a thick border.

CELL REFERENCE

■ The cell reference for the active cell appears in this area. A cell reference defines the location of each cell in a worksheet and consists of a column letter followed by a row number (example: **A1**).

1 To make another cell the active cell, move the mouse ⊕ over the cell and then press the left mouse button.

Note: To move one cell in any direction by using your keyboard, press ←, →, ↑ *or* ↓.

■ The cell reference for the active cell appears in this area.

ENTER DATA

You can enter data into your worksheet quickly and easily.

ENTER DATA

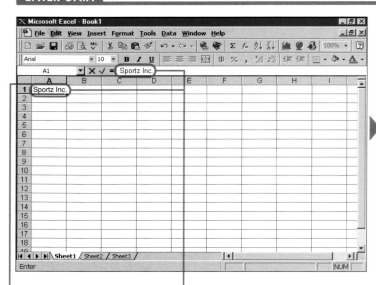

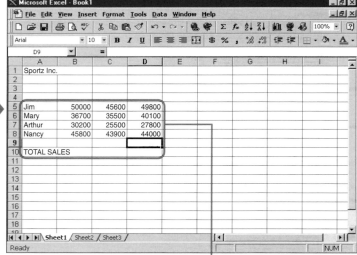

1 Move the mouse ⊕ over the cell where you want to enter data and then press the left mouse button. Then type the data.

■ If you make a typing mistake, press **◆Backspace** on your keyboard to remove the incorrect data and then type the correct data.

■ The data you type appears in the active cell and in the formula bar.

2 To enter the data and move down one cell, press **Enter** on your keyboard.

Note: To enter the data and move one cell in any direction, press ↑ , ↓ , ← *or* → *on your keyboard.*

3 Repeat steps **1** and **2** until you finish entering all the data.

How do I use the number keys on the right side of my keyboard?

When **NUM** appears at the bottom of your screen, you can use the number keys on the right side of your keyboard to enter numbers.

NUM

■ To turn the display of **NUM** on or off, press [Num Lock] on your keyboard.

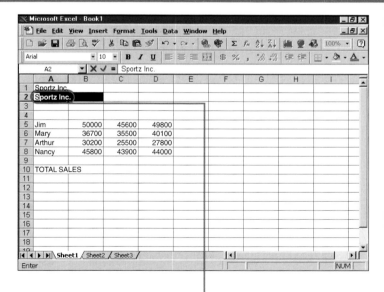

AUTOCOMPLETE

If the first few letters you type match another cell in the column, Excel will complete the text for you.

■ To keep the text Excel provides, press [Enter] on your keyboard.

■ To enter different text, continue typing.

4	TOTAL SALES	
5		
6		

4	TOTAL SA	227
5		
6		

Long Words

If text is too long to fit in a cell, the text will spill into the neighboring cell.

If the neighboring cell contains data, Excel will display as much of the text as the column width will allow. To change the column width, refer to page 90.

4	1.22E+10	
5		
6		

4	#####	
5		
6		

Long Numbers

If a number is too long to fit in a cell, Excel will display the number in scientific form or as number signs (#). To change the column width, refer to page 90.

Excel can save you time by completing a text or number series for you.

Text Series

Mon	Tue	Wed	Thu
Product 1	Product 2	Product 3	Product 4
1st Quarter	2nd Quarter	3rd Quarter	4th Quarter

■ Excel completes a text series based on the text in the first cell.

Number Series

1995	1996	1997	1998
5	10	15	20
202	204	206	208

■ Excel completes a number series based on the numbers in the first two cells.

These numbers tell Excel how much to add to each number to complete the series.

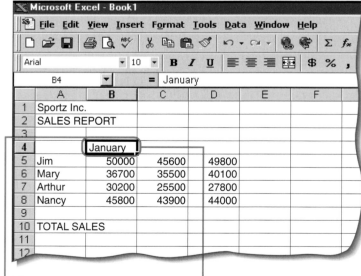

1 Enter the text or the first two numbers you want to start the series.

2 Select the cell(s) containing the text or numbers you entered. To select cells, refer to page 16.

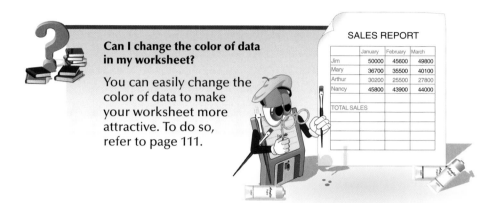

Can I change the color of data in my worksheet?

You can easily change the color of data to make your worksheet more attractive. To do so, refer to page 111.

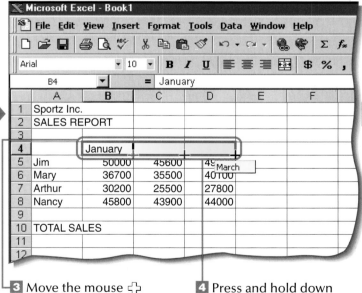

3 Move the mouse ⊹ over the bottom right corner of the cell(s) (⊹ changes to ✚).

4 Press and hold down the left mouse button as you move the mouse ✚ over the cells you want to include in the series. Then release the mouse button.

■ The cells display the series.

Note: You can also perform steps 1 to 4 to complete a series in a column.

SELECT CELLS

Before performing many tasks in Excel, you must select the cells you want to work with. Selected cells appear highlighted on your screen.

SELECT ONE CELL

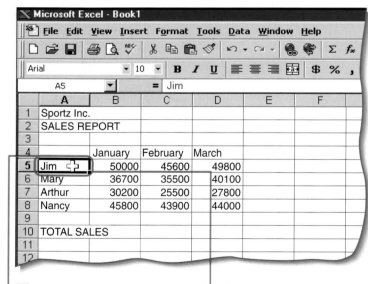

1 Move the mouse ✛ over the cell you want to select and then press the left mouse button.

■ The cell becomes the active cell and displays a thick border.

SELECT GROUPS OF CELLS

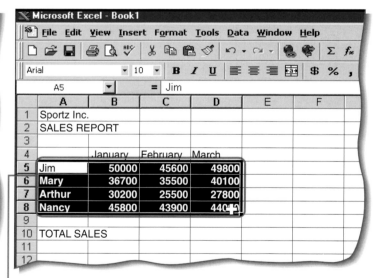

1 Move the mouse ✛ over the first cell you want to select.

2 Press and hold down the left mouse button as you move the mouse ✛ to highlight all the cells you want to select. Then release the mouse button.

■ To select multiple groups of cells, press and hold down **Ctrl** on your keyboard as you repeat steps **1** and **2** for each group.

■ To deselect cells, move the mouse ✛ over any cell and then press the left mouse button.

How do I select all the cells in my worksheet?

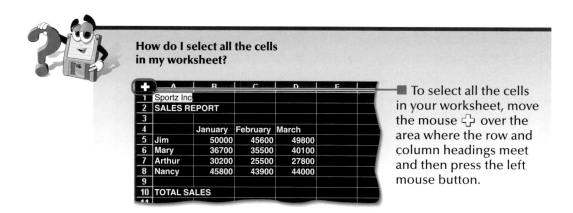

■ To select all the cells in your worksheet, move the mouse ⊕ over the area where the row and column headings meet and then press the left mouse button.

SELECT A ROW

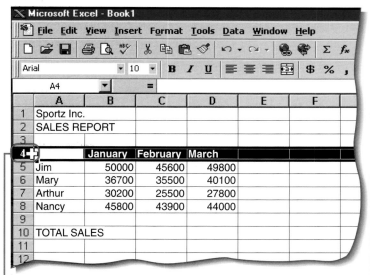

1 Move the mouse ⊕ over the number of the row you want to select and then press the left mouse button.

SELECT A COLUMN

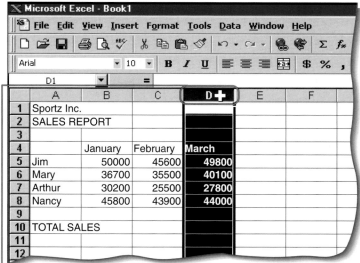

1 Move the mouse ⊕ over the letter of the column you want to select and then press the left mouse button.

SCROLL THROUGH A WORKSHEET

If your worksheet contains a lot of data, your computer screen cannot display all the data at once. You must scroll through the worksheet to view other areas.

SCROLL UP OR DOWN

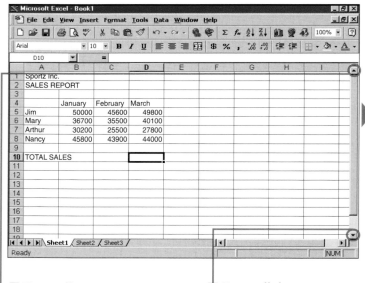

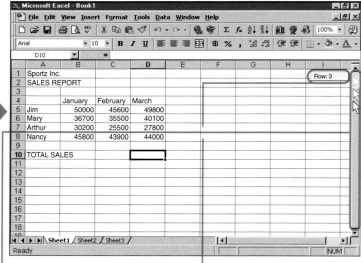

■ To scroll up one row, move the mouse ⟋ over ▲ and then press the left mouse button.

■ To scroll down one row, move the mouse ⟋ over ▼ and then press the left mouse button.

QUICKLY SCROLL

1 To quickly scroll to any row in your worksheet, move the mouse ⟋ over the scroll box.

2 Press and hold down the left mouse button as you move the mouse ⟋ up or down the scroll bar.

3 When this box displays the number of the row you want to view, release the mouse button.

How do I use the new Microsoft IntelliMouse to scroll through a worksheet?

The Microsoft IntelliMouse has a wheel between the left and right mouse buttons. Moving this wheel lets you quickly scroll up and down through a worksheet.

SCROLL LEFT OR RIGHT

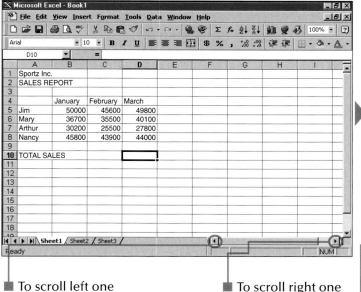

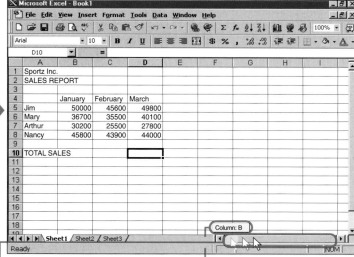

■ To scroll left one column, move the mouse over ◀ and then press the left mouse button.

■ To scroll right one column, move the mouse over ▶ and then press the left mouse button.

QUICKLY SCROLL

1 To quickly scroll to any column in your worksheet, move the mouse over the scroll box.

2 Press and hold down the left mouse button as you move the mouse left or right along the scroll bar.

3 When this box displays the letter of the column you want to view, release the mouse button.

GETTING HELP

> If you do not know how to perform a task you can ask the Office Assistant for help.

GETTING HELP

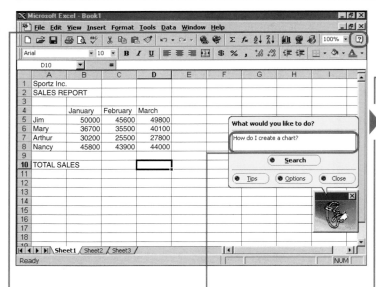

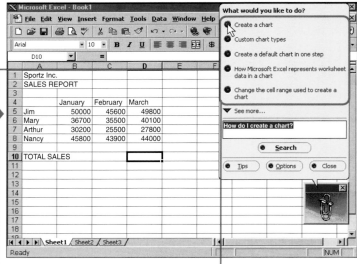

1 To display the Office Assistant, move the mouse ⍦ over [?] and then press the left mouse button.

2 Type the question you want to ask and then press **Enter** on your keyboard.

■ The Office Assistant displays a list of help topics that relate to the question you asked.

*Note: If you do not see a help topic of interest, try rephrasing your question. Type the new question and then press **Enter** on your keyboard.*

3 Move the mouse ⍦ over the help topic you want information on and then press the left mouse button.

How do I display the name of each toolbar button?

To display the name of a toolbar button, move the mouse ↳ over the button. After a few seconds, the name of the button appears.

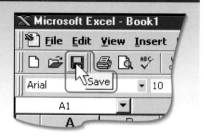

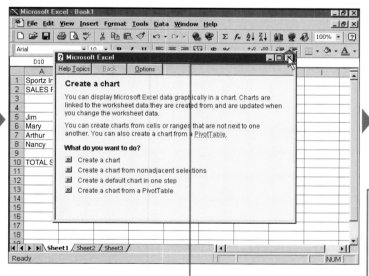

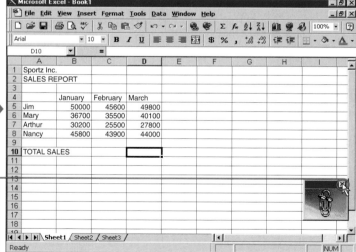

■ A window appears, displaying information about the topic you selected.

4 When you finish reading the information, move the mouse ↳ over ☒ and then press the left mouse button to close the window.

5 To hide the Office Assistant, move the mouse ↳ over ☒ and then press the left mouse button.

CHAPTER 2

SAVE AND OPEN YOUR WORKBOOKS

Are you wondering how to save, close and open an Excel workbook? Do you want to create a new workbook? Learn how in this chapter.

SAVE A WORKBOOK

You should save your workbook to store it for future use. This lets you later review and make changes to the workbook.

SAVE A WORKBOOK

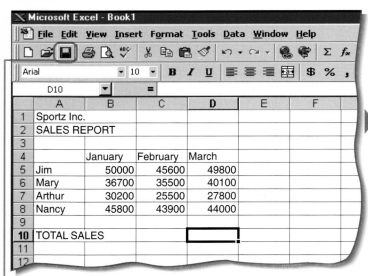

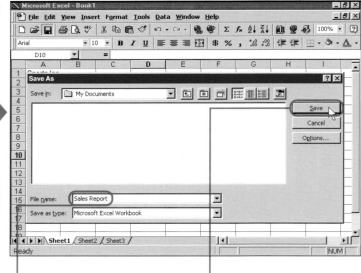

1 Move the mouse ⬚ over 🖫 and then press the left mouse button.

■ The **Save As** dialog box appears.

*Note: If you previously saved your workbook, the **Save As** dialog box will not appear since you have already named the workbook.*

2 Type a name for your workbook.

Note: You can use up to 218 characters, including spaces, to name a workbook.

3 Move the mouse ⬚ over **Save** and then press the left mouse button.

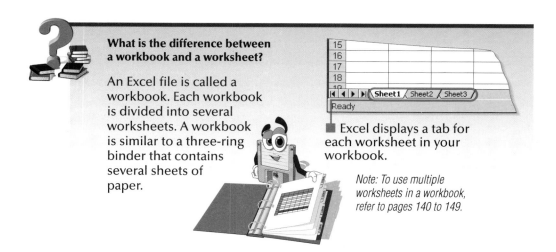

What is the difference between a workbook and a worksheet?

An Excel file is called a workbook. Each workbook is divided into several worksheets. A workbook is similar to a three-ring binder that contains several sheets of paper.

■ Excel displays a tab for each worksheet in your workbook.

Note: To use multiple worksheets in a workbook, refer to pages 140 to 149.

■ Excel saves your workbook and displays the name at the top of your screen.

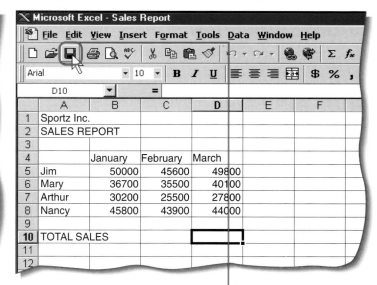

SAVE CHANGES

To avoid losing your work, you should regularly save changes you make to a workbook.

1 Move the mouse ☐ over 🖫 and then press the left mouse button.

CREATE A NEW WORKBOOK

You can easily create another workbook to store new data.

CREATE A NEW WORKBOOK

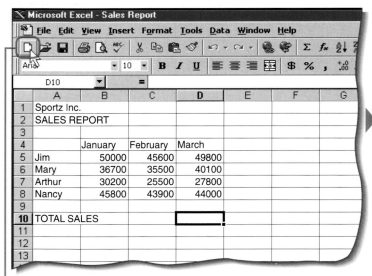

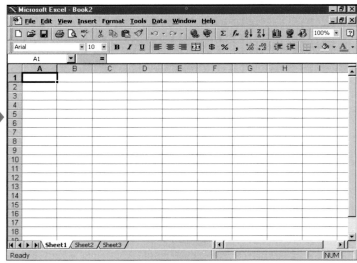

1 Move the mouse over ☐ and then press the left mouse button.

■ A new workbook appears. The previous workbook is now hidden behind the new workbook.

Excel lets you have many workbooks open at once. You can easily switch between all of your open workbooks.

SWITCH BETWEEN WORKBOOKS

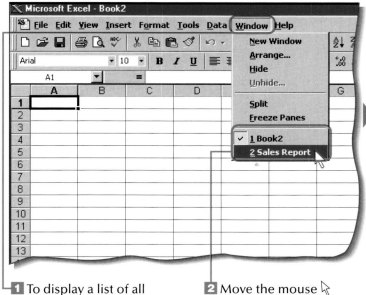

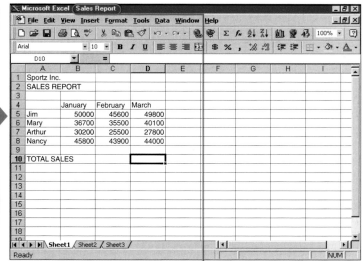

1 To display a list of all open workbooks, move the mouse over **Window** and then press the left mouse button.

2 Move the mouse over the workbook you want to display and then press the left mouse button.

■ The workbook appears.

■ Excel displays the name of the workbook at the top of your screen.

You can view the contents of all your open workbooks at the same time.

VIEW ALL OPEN WORKBOOKS

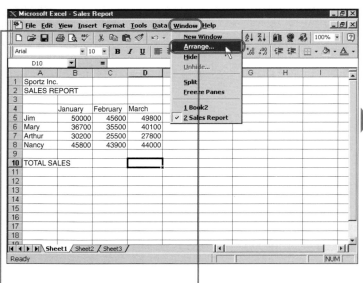

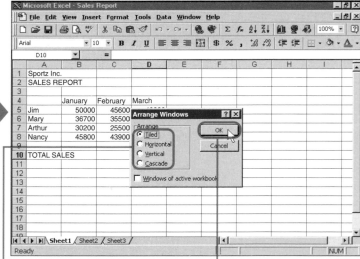

1 Move the mouse ⩗ over **Window** and then press the left mouse button.

2 Move the mouse ⩗ over **Arrange** and then press the left mouse button.

■ The **Arrange Windows** dialog box appears.

3 Move the mouse ⩗ over the way you want to arrange all your open workbooks and then press the left mouse button (○ changes to ◉).

4 Move the mouse ⩗ over **OK** and then press the left mouse button.

How can I arrange my open workbooks?

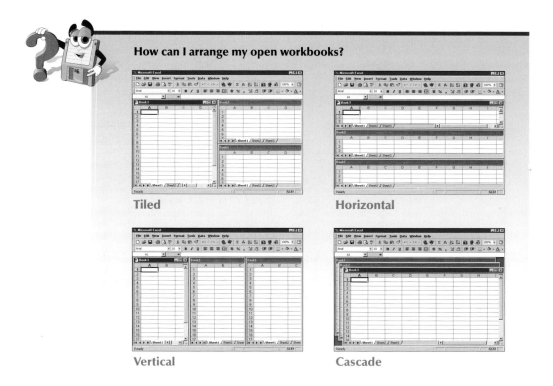

Tiled

Horizontal

Vertical

Cascade

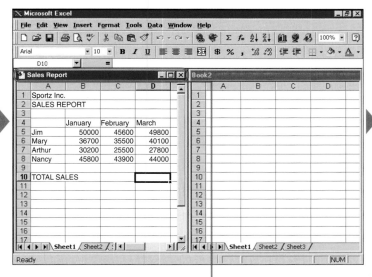

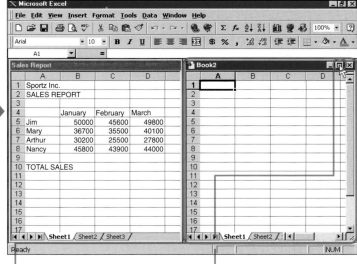

■ You can now view the contents of all your open workbooks.

■ You can only work in the current workbook, which displays a highlighted title bar.

5 To make another workbook current, move the mouse ⇖ anywhere over the workbook and then press the left mouse button.

■ To enlarge the current workbook to fill your screen, move the mouse ⇖ over ▣ and then press the left mouse button.

CLOSE A WORKBOOK

When you finish using a workbook, you can close the workbook to remove it from your screen.

When you close a workbook, you do not exit the Excel program. You can continue to work with other workbooks.

CLOSE A WORKBOOK

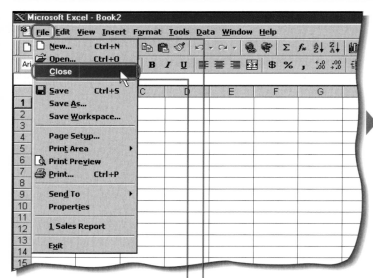

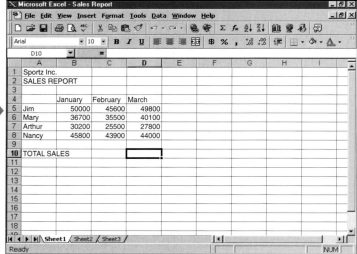

■ To save the workbook before closing, refer to page 24.

1 To close the workbook, move the mouse ⌖ over **File** and then press the left mouse button.

2 Move the mouse ⌖ over **Close** and then press the left mouse button.

■ Excel removes the workbook from your screen.

■ If you had more than one workbook open, the second last workbook you worked with appears on your screen.

When you finish using Excel, you can exit the program.

You should exit all programs before turning off your computer.

EXIT EXCEL

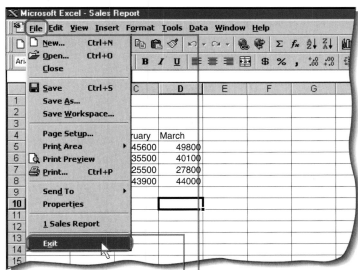

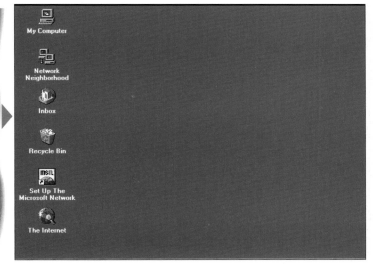

■ Save all open workbooks before exiting Excel. To save a workbook, refer to page 24.

1 Move the mouse over **File** and then press the left mouse button.

2 Move the mouse over **Exit** and then press the left mouse button.

■ The Excel window disappears from your screen.

Note: To restart Excel, refer to page 8.

OPEN A WORKBOOK

You can open a saved workbook and display it on your screen. This lets you review and make changes to the workbook.

OPEN A WORKBOOK

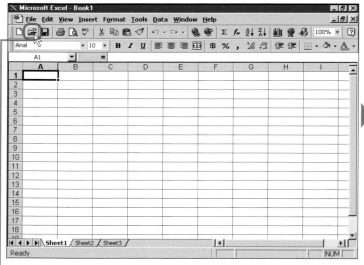

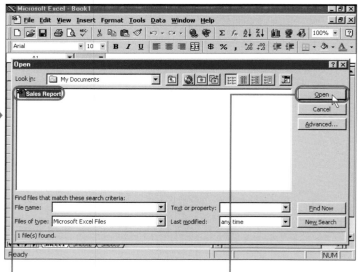

1 Move the mouse ⬚ over 📂 and then press the left mouse button.

■ The **Open** dialog box appears.

2 Move the mouse ⬚ over the name of the workbook you want to open and then press the left mouse button.

3 To open the workbook, move the mouse ⬚ over **Open** and then press the left mouse button.

32

Excel remembers the names of the last four workbooks you opened. You can quickly open any of these workbooks.

QUICKLY OPEN A WORKBOOK

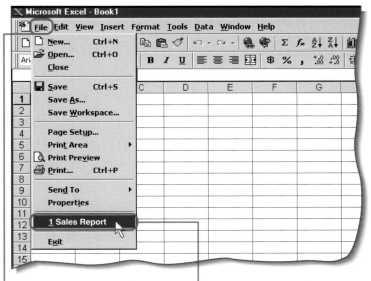

■ Excel opens the workbook and displays it on your screen. You can now review and make changes to the workbook.

■ The name of the workbook appears at the top of your screen.

1 Move the mouse ᗷ over **File** and then press the left mouse button.

2 Move the mouse ᗷ over the name of the workbook you want to open and then press the left mouse button.

FIND A WORKBOOK

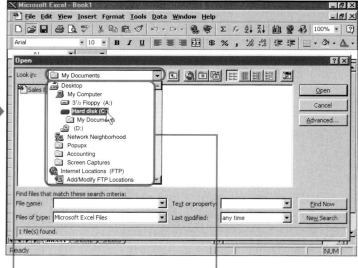

If you cannot remember the name or location of a workbook you want to open, you can search for the workbook.

FIND A WORKBOOK

1 Move the mouse over ☑ and then press the left mouse button.

■ The **Open** dialog box appears.

2 To specify where you want to search for the workbook, move the mouse over this area and then press the left mouse button.

3 Move the mouse over the location you want to search and then press the left mouse button.

34

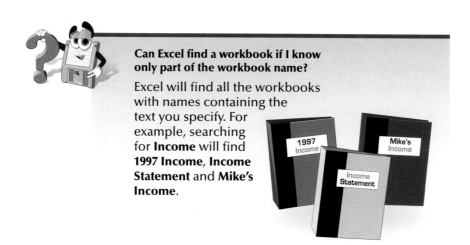

Can Excel find a workbook if I know only part of the workbook name?

Excel will find all the workbooks with names containing the text you specify. For example, searching for **Income** will find **1997 Income**, **Income Statement** and **Mike's Income**.

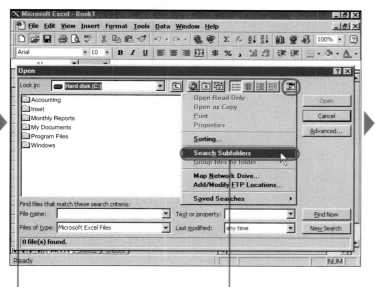

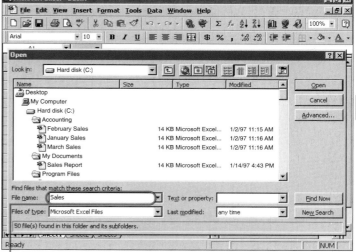

4 To search the contents of all the folders in the location you selected, move the mouse ↖ over 🔢 and then press the left mouse button.

5 Move the mouse ↖ over **Search Subfolders** and then press the left mouse button.

6 If you know part or all of the name of the workbook you want to find, move the mouse I over this area and then press the left mouse button. Then type the name.

CONTINUED➡

FIND A WORKBOOK

When the search is complete, Excel displays the names of the workbooks it found.

> **Expenses**
> **Sales Meeting**
> **1997 Conference**
> **Budget**

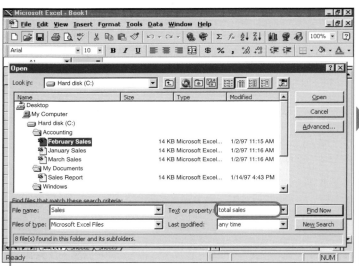

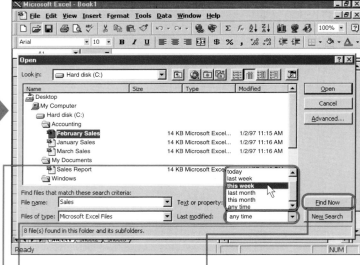

7 If you know a word or phrase in the workbook you want to find, move the mouse I over this area and then press the left mouse button. Then type the word or phrase.

8 If you know when you last saved the workbook you want to find, move the mouse ⬚ over this area and then press the left mouse button.

9 Move the mouse ⬚ over the appropriate time period and then press the left mouse button.

10 To complete the search, move the mouse ⬚ over **Find Now** and then press the left mouse button.

How can Excel help me find a workbook?

There are many ways you can search for a workbook.

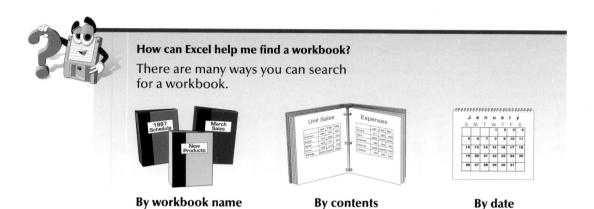

By workbook name   **By contents**   **By date**

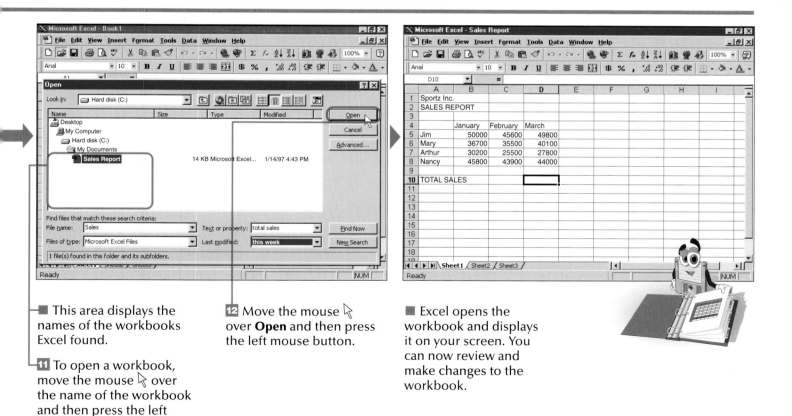

■ This area displays the names of the workbooks Excel found.

11 To open a workbook, move the mouse ⬓ over the name of the workbook and then press the left mouse button.

12 Move the mouse ⬓ over **Open** and then press the left mouse button.

■ Excel opens the workbook and displays it on your screen. You can now review and make changes to the workbook.

CHAPTER 3

EDIT YOUR WORKSHEETS

Do you want to edit the data in your worksheet? Are you wondering how to check for spelling errors? This chapter teaches you how.

You can easily change your data to correct a mistake or update the data.

EDIT DATA

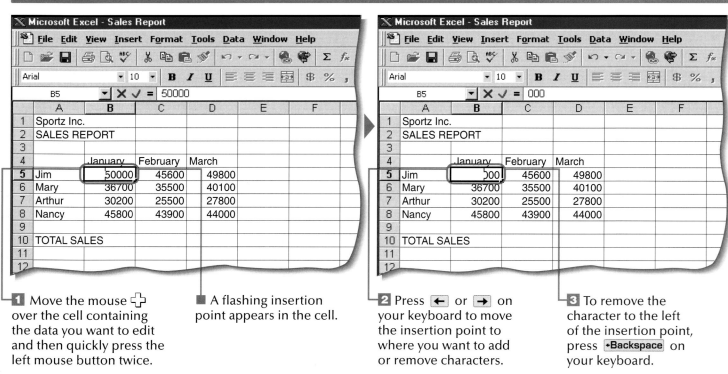

1 Move the mouse ⊕ over the cell containing the data you want to edit and then quickly press the left mouse button twice.

■ A flashing insertion point appears in the cell.

2 Press ← or → on your keyboard to move the insertion point to where you want to add or remove characters.

3 To remove the character to the left of the insertion point, press **◆Backspace** on your keyboard.

How often should I save my workbook?

You should save your workbook every 5 to 10 minutes to avoid losing your editing changes. To save a workbook, refer to page 24.

REPLACE ALL DATA IN A CELL

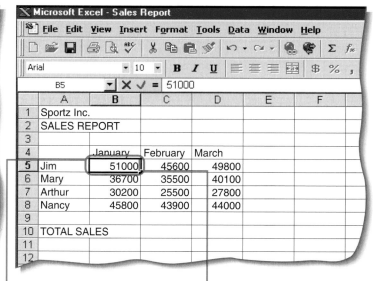

4 To insert data where the insertion point flashes on your screen, type the data.

5 When you finish making changes to the data, press **Enter** on your keyboard.

1 Move the mouse ⊹ over the cell containing the data you want to replace with new data and then press the left mouse button.

2 Type the new data and then press **Enter** on your keyboard.

DELETE DATA

You can easily remove data you no longer need from cells in your worksheet.

DELETE DATA

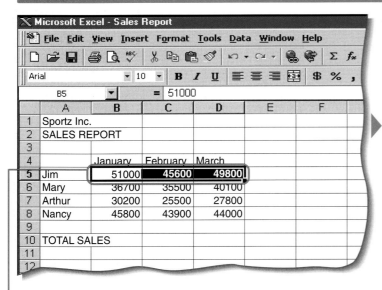

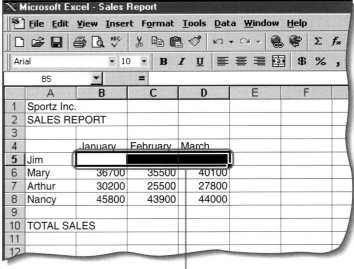

1 Select the cell(s) containing the data you want to delete. To select cells, refer to page 16.

2 Press `Delete` on your keyboard.

■ The data in the cell(s) you selected disappears.

UNDO LAST CHANGE

Excel remembers the last changes you made to your worksheet. If you regret these changes, you can undo them.

UNDO LAST CHANGE

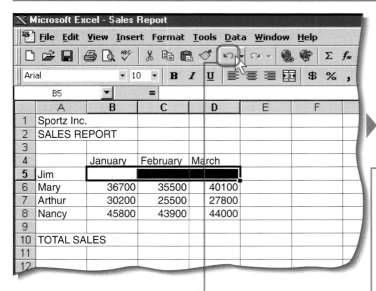

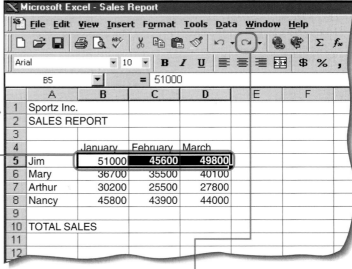

The Undo feature can cancel your last editing and formatting changes.

1 To undo your last change, move the mouse over [↶] and then press the left mouse button.

■ Excel cancels the last change you made to your worksheet.

■ You can repeat step **1** to cancel previous changes you made.

■ To reverse the results of using the Undo feature, move the mouse over [↷] and then press the left mouse button.

MOVE DATA

You can reorganize the data in your worksheet by moving data from one location to another.

MOVE DATA

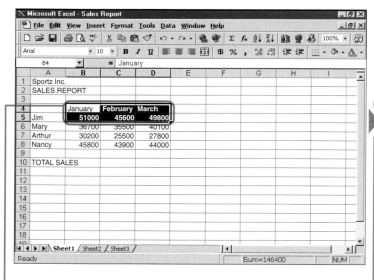

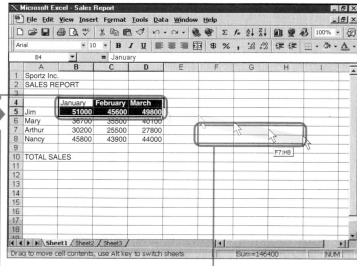

1 Select the cells containing the data you want to move. To select cells, refer to page 16.

2 Move the mouse ⊕ over a border of the selected cells (⊕ changes to ↖).

3 Press and hold down the left mouse button as you move the mouse ↖ to where you want to place the data.

Why does this message appear when I try to move data?

This message may appear when you try to move data to a location that already contains data.

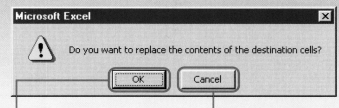

■ If you want Excel to replace the existing data with the data you are moving, move the mouse ⫯ over **OK** and then press the left mouse button.

■ To cancel the move, move the mouse ⫯ over **Cancel** and then press the left mouse button.

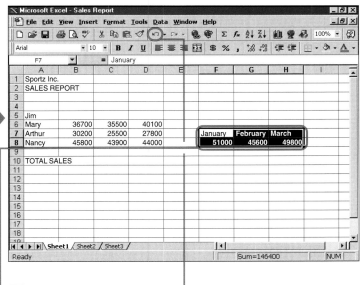

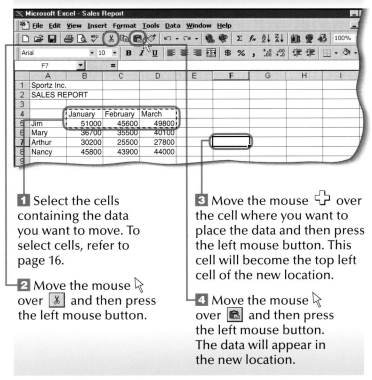

MOVE DATA USING TOOLBAR BUTTONS

4 Release the mouse button and the data moves to the new location.

UNDO THE MOVE

■ To immediately move the data back, move the mouse ⫯ over ◄⎯ and then press the left mouse button.

1 Select the cells containing the data you want to move. To select cells, refer to page 16.

2 Move the mouse ⫯ over ✂ and then press the left mouse button.

3 Move the mouse ⊹ over the cell where you want to place the data and then press the left mouse button. This cell will become the top left cell of the new location.

4 Move the mouse ⫯ over 📋 and then press the left mouse button. The data will appear in the new location.

COPY DATA

You can place a copy of data in a different location in your worksheet. This will save you time since you do not have to retype the data.

COPY DATA

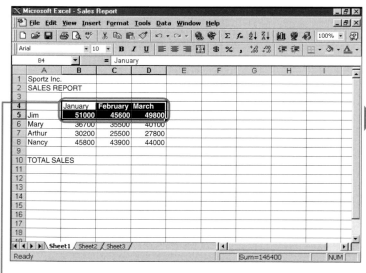

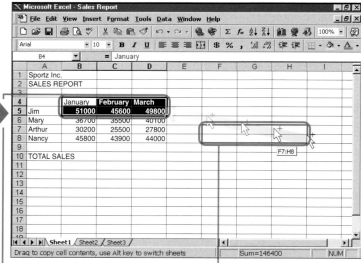

1 Select the cells containing the data you want to copy. To select cells, refer to page 16.

2 Move the mouse ✛ over a border of the selected cells (✛ changes to ↖).

3 Press and hold down **Ctrl** on your keyboard.

4 Still holding down **Ctrl**, press and hold down the left mouse button as you move the mouse ↖ to where you want to place the copy.

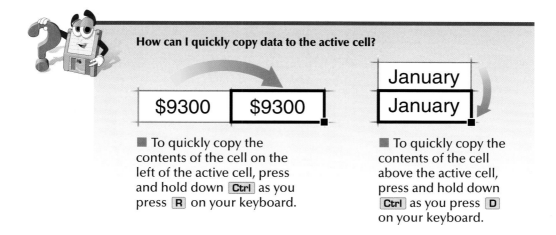

How can I quickly copy data to the active cell?

$9300 $9300

■ To quickly copy the contents of the cell on the left of the active cell, press and hold down `Ctrl` as you press `R` on your keyboard.

January
January

■ To quickly copy the contents of the cell above the active cell, press and hold down `Ctrl` as you press `D` on your keyboard.

COPY DATA USING TOOLBAR BUTTONS

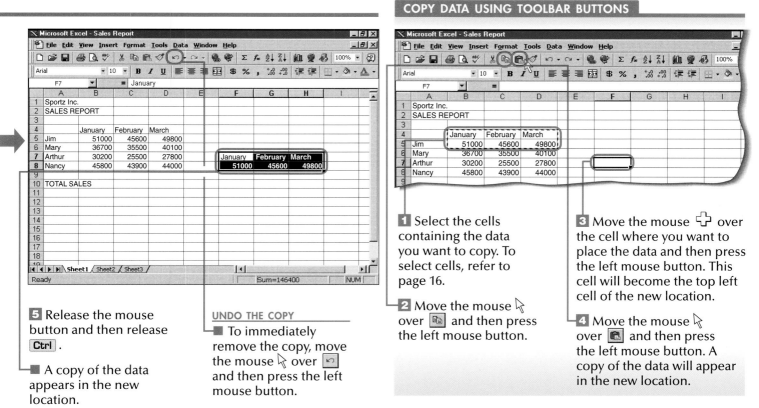

5 Release the mouse button and then release `Ctrl`.

■ A copy of the data appears in the new location.

UNDO THE COPY

■ To immediately remove the copy, move the mouse ☇ over ☜ and then press the left mouse button.

1 Select the cells containing the data you want to copy. To select cells, refer to page 16.

2 Move the mouse ☇ over 🗎 and then press the left mouse button.

3 Move the mouse ⊹ over the cell where you want to place the data and then press the left mouse button. This cell will become the top left cell of the new location.

4 Move the mouse ☇ over 🗎 and then press the left mouse button. A copy of the data will appear in the new location.

> You can quickly find and correct all the spelling errors in your worksheet.

Excel compares every word in your worksheet to words in its dictionary. If a word does not exist in the dictionary, Excel considers it misspelled.

CHECK SPELLING

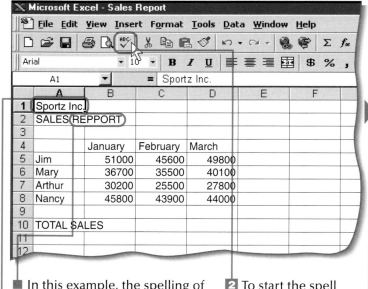

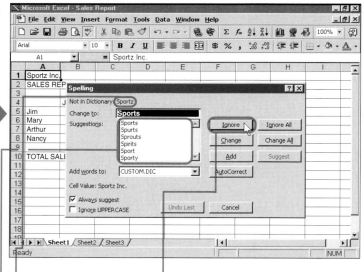

■ In this example, the spelling of **REPORT** was changed to **REPPORT**.

1 To start the spell check at the beginning of your worksheet, move the mouse ⊹ over cell **A1** and then press the left mouse button.

2 To start the spell check, move the mouse ☝ over [ABC✓] and then press the left mouse button.

■ The **Spelling** dialog box appears if Excel finds a misspelled word.

■ This area displays the first misspelled word.

■ This area displays suggestions to correct the word.

IGNORE AN ERROR

3 To ignore an error and continue checking your worksheet, move the mouse ☝ over **Ignore** and then press the left mouse button.

*Note: To ignore an error and all occurrences of the error in the worksheet, move the mouse ☝ over **Ignore All** and then press the left mouse button.*

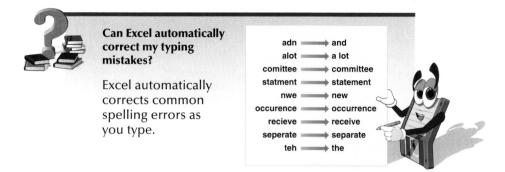

Can Excel automatically correct my typing mistakes?

Excel automatically corrects common spelling errors as you type.

adn	➞ and
alot	➞ a lot
comittee	➞ committee
statment	➞ statement
nwe	➞ new
occurence	➞ occurrence
recieve	➞ receive
seperate	➞ separate
teh	➞ the

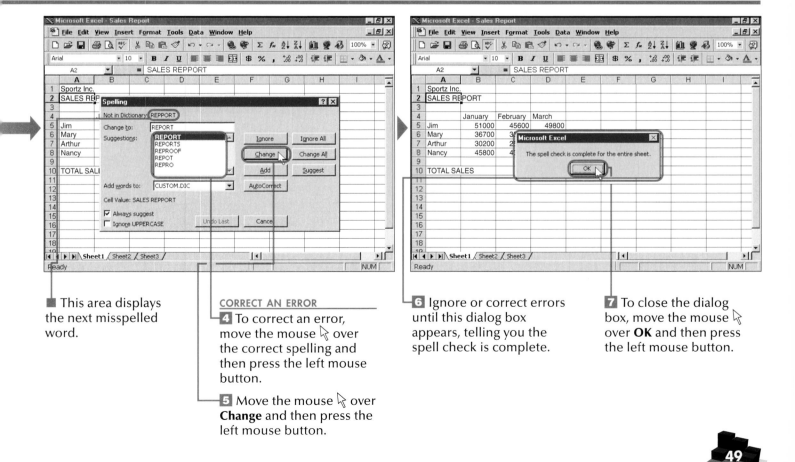

■ This area displays the next misspelled word.

CORRECT AN ERROR

4 To correct an error, move the mouse ⇖ over the correct spelling and then press the left mouse button.

5 Move the mouse ⇖ over **Change** and then press the left mouse button.

6 Ignore or correct errors until this dialog box appears, telling you the spell check is complete.

7 To close the dialog box, move the mouse ⇖ over **OK** and then press the left mouse button.

FIND DATA

You can use the Find feature to quickly locate a word or number in your worksheet.

Excel will find the data even if it is part of a larger word or number. For example, searching for 105 will find 105, 2105 and 1056.

FIND DATA

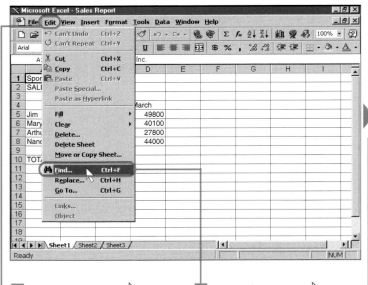

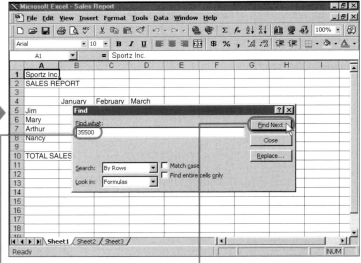

1 Move the mouse ▷ over **Edit** and then press the left mouse button.

2 Move the mouse ▷ over **Find** and then press the left mouse button.

■ The **Find** dialog box appears.

3 Type the word or number you want to find.

4 To start the search, move the mouse ▷ over **Find Next** and then press the left mouse button.

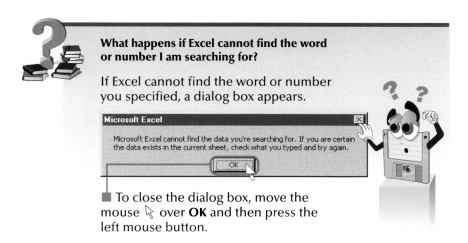

What happens if Excel cannot find the word or number I am searching for?

If Excel cannot find the word or number you specified, a dialog box appears.

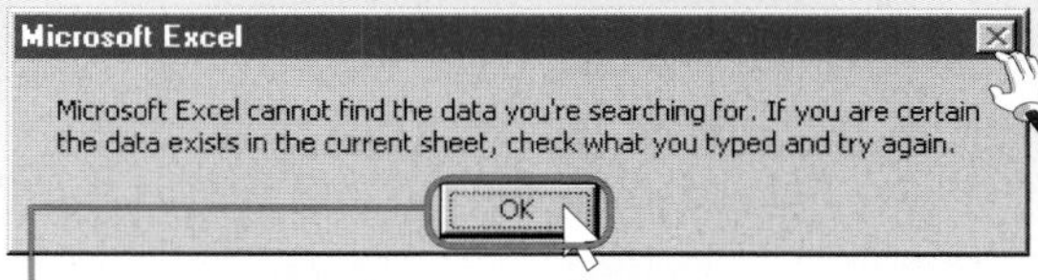

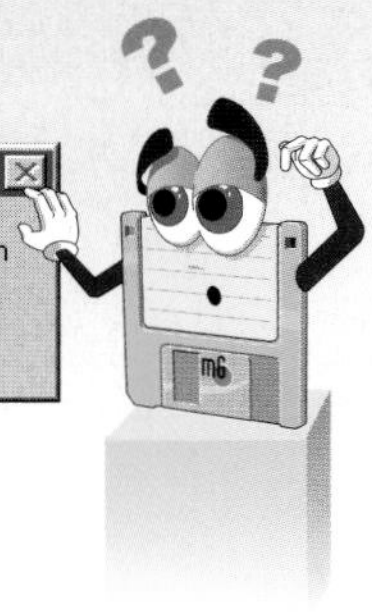

■ To close the dialog box, move the mouse over **OK** and then press the left mouse button.

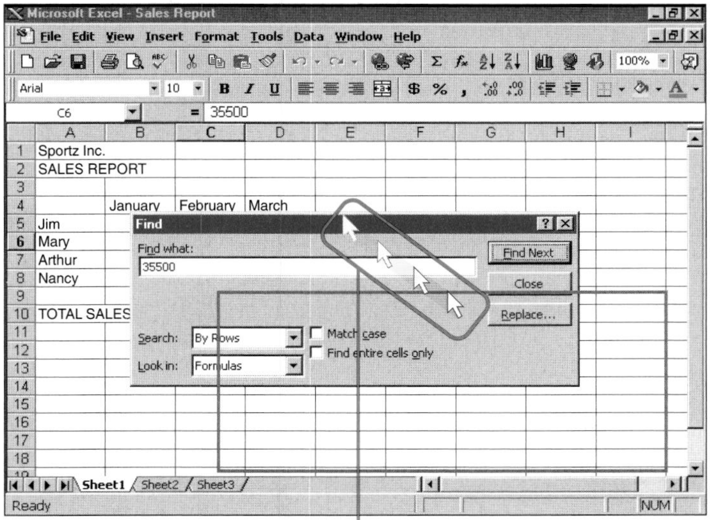

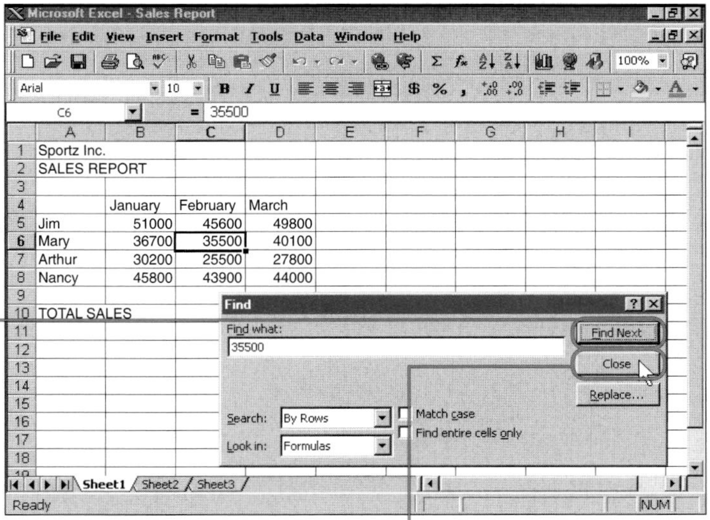

■ Excel highlights the first cell containing the word or number.

■ If the highlighted cell is hidden behind the **Find** dialog box, you can move the dialog box.

5 To move the **Find** dialog box, move the mouse over the title bar.

6 Press and hold down the left mouse button as you move the dialog box to a new location. Then release the mouse button.

7 To find the next matching word or number, move the mouse over **Find Next** and then press the left mouse button.

8 To close the dialog box, move the mouse over **Close** and then press the left mouse button.

INSERT A ROW OR COLUMN

You can add a row or column to your worksheet when you want to insert additional data.

	Week 1	Week 2	Week 3
Apples	45	30	35
Bananas	50	75	85
Grapes	20	120	45
Lemons	65	70	90
Limes	80	70	55
Mangoes	40	50	45
Oranges	50	90	65
Peaches	30	110	35
Pears	60	30	80
Plums	20	65	50

INSERT A ROW

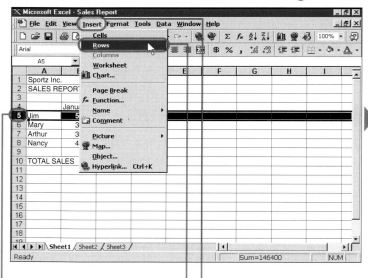

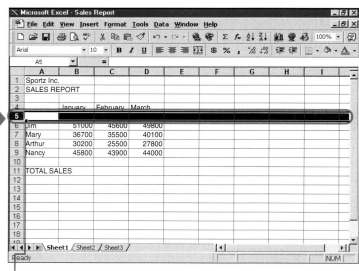

Excel will insert a row above the row you select.

1 To select a row, move the mouse ⊹ over the row number and then press the left mouse button.

2 Move the mouse ⊳ over **Insert** and then press the left mouse button.

3 Move the mouse ⊳ over **Rows** and then press the left mouse button.

■ The new row appears and all the rows that follow shift downward.

Do I need to adjust my formulas when I insert a row or column?

When you insert a row or column, Excel updates any formulas affected by the insertion.

Note: For information on formulas, refer to page 58.

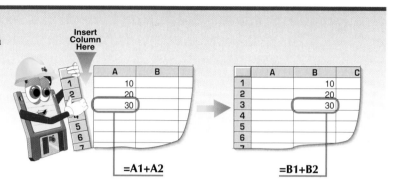

=A1+A2   =B1+B2

INSERT A COLUMN

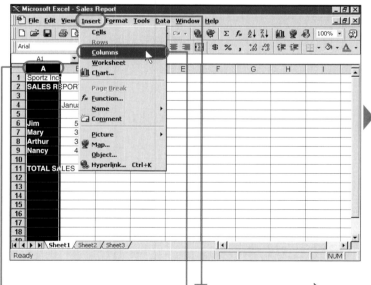

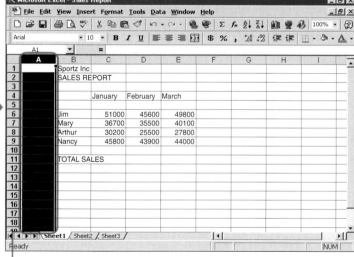

Excel will insert a column to the left of the column you select.

1 To select a column, move the mouse ⟐ over the column letter and then press the left mouse button.

2 Move the mouse ⟐ over **Insert** and then press the left mouse button.

3 Move the mouse ⟐ over **Columns** and then press the left mouse button.

■ The new column appears and all the columns that follow shift to the right.

DELETE A ROW OR COLUMN

You can delete a row or column from your worksheet to remove cells you no longer need.

DELETE A ROW

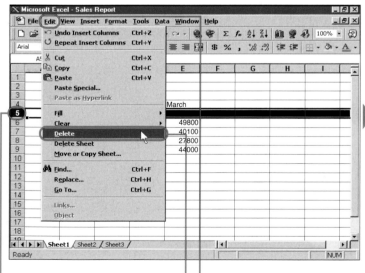

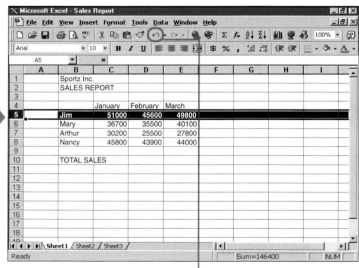

1 To select the row you want to delete, move the mouse ⊕ over the row number and then press the left mouse button.

2 Move the mouse ⌖ over **Edit** and then press the left mouse button.

3 Move the mouse ⌖ over **Delete** and then press the left mouse button.

■ The row disappears and all the rows that follow shift upward.

■ To immediately return the row to your worksheet, move the mouse ⌖ over ↶ and then press the left mouse button.

Why did #REF! appear in a cell after I deleted a row or column?

If **#REF!** appears in a cell in your worksheet, you deleted data needed to calculate a formula.

Note: For information on formulas, refer to page 58.

DELETE A COLUMN

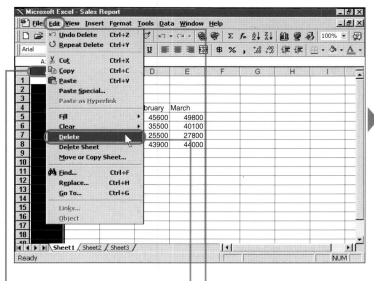

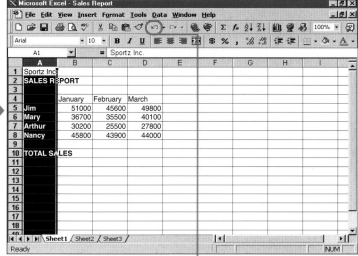

1 To select the column you want to delete, move the mouse ⊕ over the column letter and then press the left mouse button.

2 Move the mouse ⇖ over **Edit** and then press the left mouse button.

3 Move the mouse ⇖ over **Delete** and then press the left mouse button.

■ The column disappears and all the columns that follow shift to the left.

■ To immediately return the column to your worksheet, move the mouse ⇖ over 🔄 and then press the left mouse button.

CHAPTER 4

WORK WITH FORMULAS AND FUNCTIONS

Are you ready to perform calculations on the data in your worksheet? This chapter teaches you how to work with formulas and functions.

ENTER A FORMULA

A formula helps you calculate and analyze data in your worksheet.

A formula always begins with an equal sign (=).

INTRODUCTION TO FORMULAS

Order of Calculations

Excel performs calculations in the following order:

1 Exponents (^)

2 Multiplication (*) and Division (/)

3 Addition (+) and Subtraction (-)

You can use parentheses ( ) to change the order in which Excel performs calculations. Excel will calculate the data inside the parentheses first.

Cell References

When entering formulas, use cell references (example: **=A1+A2**) instead of actual data (example: **=10+30**) whenever possible. When you use cell references and you change a number used in a formula, Excel will automatically redo the calculations for you.

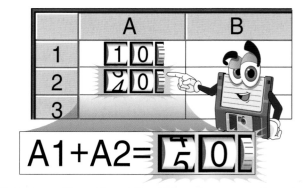

EXAMPLES OF FORMULAS

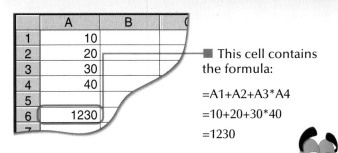

	A	B	C
1	10		
2	20		
3	30		
4	40		
5			
6	1230		

■ This cell contains the formula:

=A1+A2+A3*A4

=10+20+30*40

=1230

	A	B	C
1	10		
2	20		
3	30		
4	40		
5			
6	2010		

■ This cell contains the formula:

=A1+(A2+A3)*A4

=10+(20+30)*40

=2010

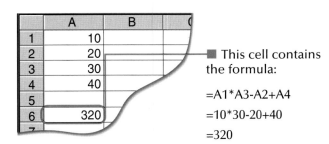

	A	B	C
1	10		
2	20		
3	30		
4	40		
5			
6	320		

■ This cell contains the formula:

=A1*A3-A2+A4

=10*30-20+40

=320

	A	B	C
1	10		
2	20		
3	30		
4	40		
5			
6	140		

■ This cell contains the formula:

=A1*(A3-A2)+A4

=10*(30-20)+40

=140

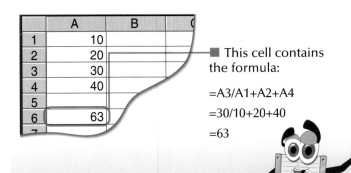

	A	B	C
1	10		
2	20		
3	30		
4	40		
5			
6	63		

■ This cell contains the formula:

=A3/A1+A2+A4

=30/10+20+40

=63

	A	B	C
1	10		
2	20		
3	30		
4	40		
5			
6	41		

■ This cell contains the formula:

=A3/(A1+A2)+A4

=30/(10+20)+40

=41

ENTER A FORMULA

mG's Pizza Parlor

ORDERS

	A	B
1	Pizza	600
2	Spaghetti	200
3	Garlic Bread	400
4	TOTAL	1200

=B1+B2+B3

You can enter a formula into any cell in your worksheet.

ENTER A FORMULA

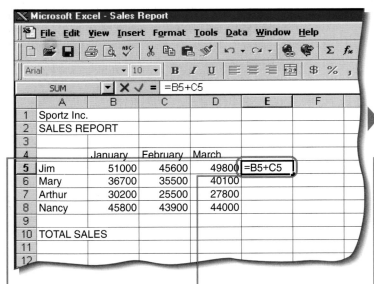

1 Move the mouse ✛ over the cell where you want to enter a formula and then press the left mouse button.

2 Type an equal sign (=) to begin the formula.

3 Type the formula and then press **Enter** on your keyboard.

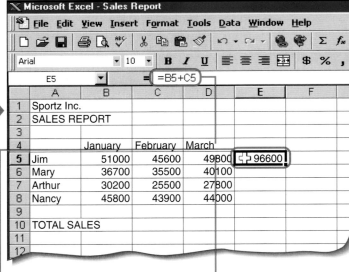

■ The result of the calculation appears in the cell.

4 To view the formula you entered, move the mouse ✛ over the cell containing the formula and then press the left mouse button.

■ The formula for the cell appears in the formula bar.

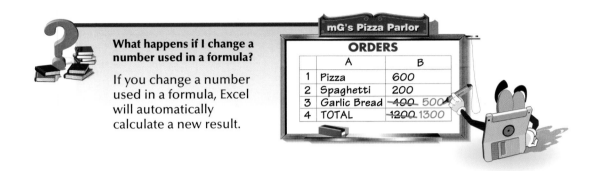

What happens if I change a number used in a formula?

If you change a number used in a formula, Excel will automatically calculate a new result.

EDIT A FORMULA

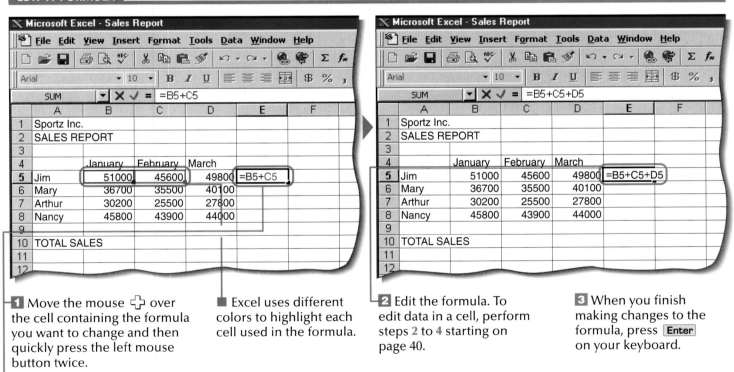

1 Move the mouse ➕ over the cell containing the formula you want to change and then quickly press the left mouse button twice.

■ The formula appears in the cell.

■ Excel uses different colors to highlight each cell used in the formula.

2 Edit the formula. To edit data in a cell, perform steps **2** to **4** starting on page 40.

3 When you finish making changes to the formula, press **Enter** on your keyboard.

ENTER A FUNCTION

A function is a ready-to-use formula that performs a specialized calculation on your worksheet data.

INTRODUCTION TO FUNCTIONS

■ A function always begins with an equal sign (=).

■ The data Excel will use to calculate a function is enclosed in parentheses ( ).

```
=SUM(A1,A2,A3)

=AVERAGE(C1,C2,C3)

=MAX(B7,C7,D7,E7)

=COUNT(D12,D13,D14)
```

```
=SUM(A1:A3)

=AVERAGE(C1:C3)

=MAX(B7:E7)

=COUNT(D12:D14)
```

Specify Individual Cells

When there is a comma (,) between cell references in a function, Excel uses each cell to perform the calculation.

For example, =SUM(A1,A2,A3) is the same as the formula =A1+A2+A3.

Specify Group of Cells

When there is a colon (:) between cell references in a function, Excel uses the specified cells and all cells between them to perform the calculation.

For example, =SUM(A1:A3) is the same as the formula =A1+A2+A3.

COMMON FUNCTIONS

	A	B	
1	10		
2	20		
3	30		
4	40		
5			
6	25		
7			

Average

Calculates the average value of a list of numbers.

■ This cell contains the function:

=AVERAGE(A1:A4)

=(A1+A2+A3+A4)/4

=(10+20+30+40)/4

=25

	A	B	
1	10		
2	20		
3	30		
4	40		
5			
6	4		
7			

Count

Calculates the number of values in a list.

■ This cell contains the function:

=COUNT(A1:A4)

=4

	A	B	
1	10		
2	20		
3	30		
4	40		
5			
6	40		
7			

Max

Finds the largest value in a list of numbers.

■ This cell contains the function:

=MAX(A1:A4)

=40

	A	B	
1	10		
2	20		
3	30		
4	40		
5			
6	10		
7			

Min

Finds the smallest value in a list of numbers.

■ This cell contains the function:

=MIN(A1:A4)

=10

	A	B	
1	10		
2	20		
3	30		
4	40		
5			
6	100		
7			

Sum

Adds a list of numbers.

■ This cell contains the function:

=SUM(A1:A4)

=A1+A2+A3+A4

=10+20+30+40

=100

	A	B	
1	42.3617		
2			
3			
4			
5			
6	42.36		
7			

Round

Rounds a value to a specific number of digits.

■ This cell contains the function:

=ROUND(A1,2)

=42.36

ENTER A FUNCTION

Excel helps you enter functions in your worksheet. This lets you perform calculations without typing long, complex formulas.

ENTER A FUNCTION

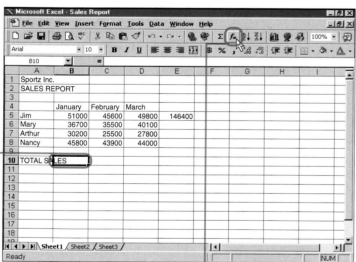

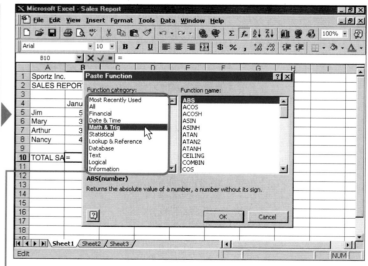

1 Move the mouse ⊕ over the cell where you want to enter a function and then press the left mouse button.

2 Move the mouse ⌖ over ![fx] and then press the left mouse button.

■ The **Paste Function** dialog box appears.

3 Move the mouse ⌖ over the category that contains the function you want to use and then press the left mouse button.

*Note: If you do not know which category contains the function you want to use, select **All** to display a list of all the functions.*

How many functions does Excel offer?

Excel offers over 200 functions to help you analyze data in your worksheet. There are financial functions, math and trigonometry functions, date and time functions, statistical functions and many more.

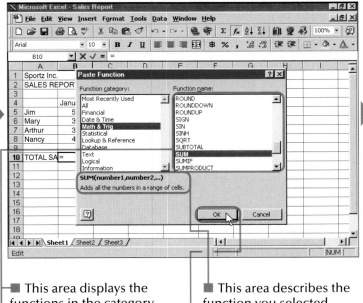

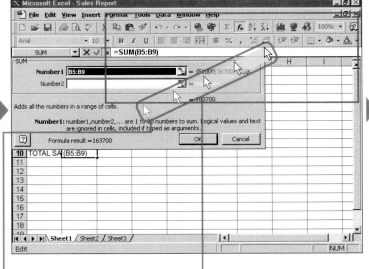

■ This area displays the functions in the category you selected.

4 Move the mouse ↳ over a function of interest and then press the left mouse button.

■ This area describes the function you selected.

5 To enter the function in your worksheet, move the mouse ↳ over **OK** and then press the left mouse button.

■ A dialog box appears. If the dialog box covers data you want to use in the calculation, you can move it to a new location.

6 To move the dialog box, move the mouse ↳ over a blank area in the dialog box.

7 Press and hold down the left mouse button as you move the dialog box to a new location. Then release the mouse button.

CONTINUED➡

When entering a function, you must specify which numbers you want to use in the calculation.

=SUM(D1:D4)

	A	B	C	D
1	100	12	128	20
2	200	22	601	60
3	400	68	288	80
4	800	21	204	97

ENTER A FUNCTION (CONTINUED)

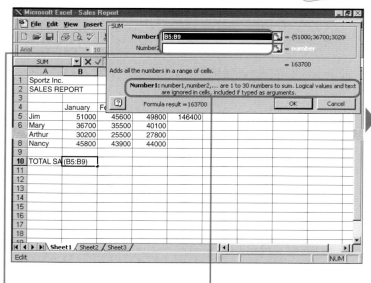

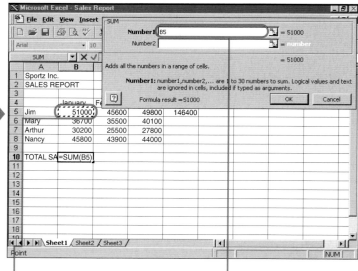

■ This area displays boxes where you enter the numbers you want to use in the calculation.

■ This area describes the number you need to enter.

8 To enter a number, move the mouse ⊹ over the cell in your worksheet containing the number and then press the left mouse button.

Note: If the number you want to enter does not appear in the worksheet, type the number.

■ This area now displays the cell you selected.

Can I enter a function by myself?

You can easily enter a function yourself by typing the entire function into a cell.

=COUNT(D1:D▮

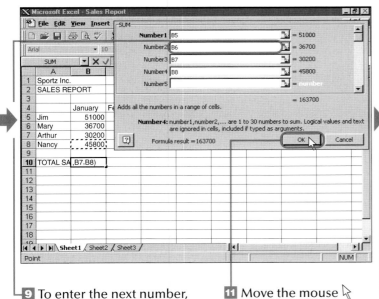

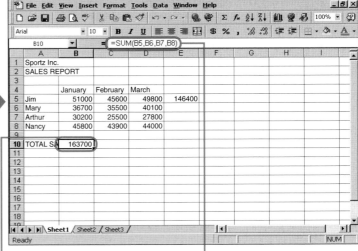

■■ **9** To enter the next number, move the mouse I over the next area and then press the left mouse button.

10 Repeat steps **8** and **9** until you have entered all the numbers you want to use in the calculation.

11 Move the mouse ⌖ over **OK** and then press the left mouse button.

■ The result of the function appears in the cell.

■ The function for the active cell appears in the formula bar.

USING AUTOCALCULATE

You can quickly view the results of common calculations without entering a formula into your worksheet.

USING AUTOCALCULATE

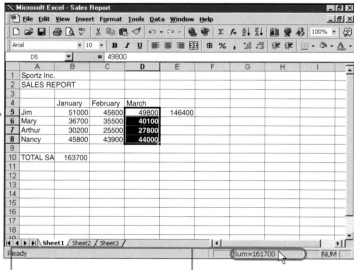

1 Select the cells you want to include in the calculation. To select cells, refer to page 16.

■ This area displays the sum of the cells you selected.

2 To display the result for a different calculation, move the mouse ⇗ over this area and then press the **right** mouse button.

What calculations can AutoCalculate perform?

Average
Calculates the average value of a list of numbers.

Count
Calculates the number of items in a list, including text.

Count Nums
Calculates the number of values in a list.

Max
Finds the largest value in a list.

Min
Finds the smallest value in a list.

Sum
Adds a list of numbers.

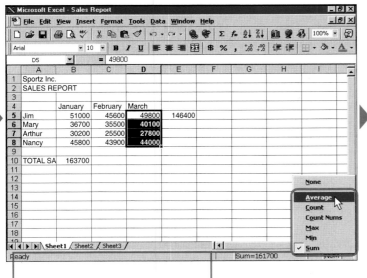

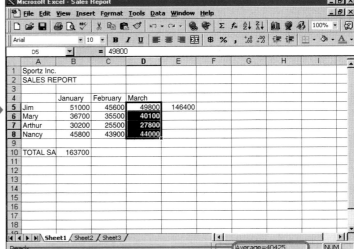

■ A list appears, displaying the calculations you can perform.

3 Move the mouse over the calculation you want to perform and then press the left mouse button.

■ This area displays the result for the new calculation.

ADD NUMBERS

You can quickly add a list of numbers in your worksheet.

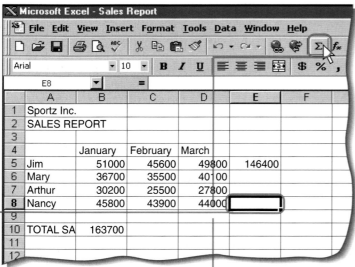

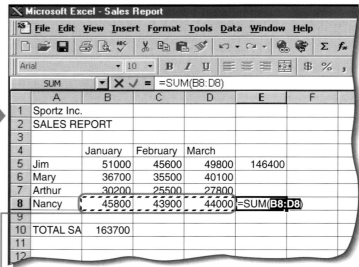

1 Move the mouse ✛ over the cell below or to the right of the cells you want to add and then press the left mouse button.

2 Move the mouse ◊ over Σ and then press the left mouse button.

■ Excel outlines the cells it will use in the calculation with a dotted line.

■ If Excel does not outline the correct cells, select the cells containing the numbers you want to add. To select cells, refer to page 16.

If your worksheet contains several subtotals, you can quickly calculate a grand total.

CALCULATE A GRAND TOTAL

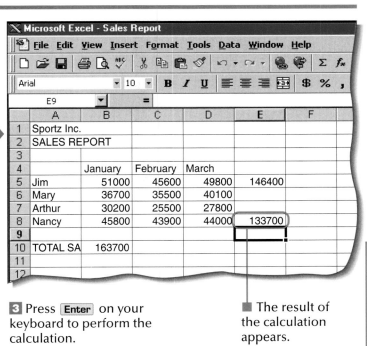

Microsoft Excel - Sales Report

File Edit View Insert Format Tools Data Window Help

Arial   10

E9   =

	A	B	C	D	E	F
1	Sportz Inc.					
2	SALES REPORT					
3						
4		January	February	March		
5	Jim	51000	45600	49800	146400	
6	Mary	36700	35500	40100		
7	Arthur	30200	25500	27800		
8	Nancy	45800	43900	44000	133700	
9						
10	TOTAL SA	163700				
11						
12						

3 Press **Enter** on your keyboard to perform the calculation.

■ The result of the calculation appears.

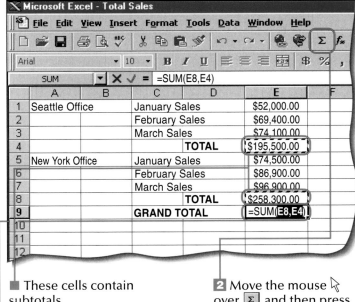

Microsoft Excel - Total Sales

File Edit View Insert Format Tools Data Window Help

Arial   10

SUM   ✕ ✓ =   =SUM(E8,E4)

	A	B	C	D	E	F
1	Seattle Office		January Sales		$52,000.00	
2			February Sales		$69,400.00	
3			March Sales		$74,100.00	
4				TOTAL	$195,500.00	
5	New York Office		January Sales		$74,500.00	
6			February Sales		$86,900.00	
7			March Sales		$96,900.00	
8				TOTAL	$258,300.00	
9			GRAND TOTAL		=SUM(E8,E4)	
10						
11						
12						

■ These cells contain subtotals.

1 Move the mouse ⊹ over the cell below or to the right of the cells containing the subtotals and then press the left mouse button.

2 Move the mouse ⤢ over **Σ** and then press the left mouse button.

3 Press **Enter** on your keyboard.

ERRORS IN FORMULAS

An error message appears when Excel cannot properly calculate a formula.

Errors in formulas are often the result of typing mistakes. You can correct an error by editing the cell containing the error. To edit data in a cell, refer to page 40.

#####

The column is too narrow to display the result of the calculation. To display the result, refer to page 90 to change the column width.

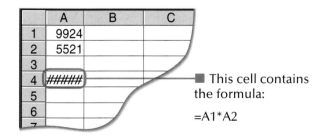

	A	B	C
1	9924		
2	5521		
3			
4	#####		
5			
6			

■ This cell contains the formula:

=A1*A2

#DIV/0!

The formula divides a number by zero (0). Excel considers a blank cell to contain a value of zero.

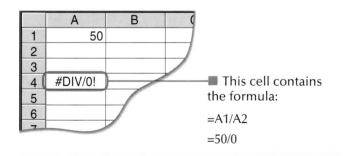

	A	B	
1	50		
2			
3			
4	#DIV/0!		
5			
6			

■ This cell contains the formula:

=A1/A2

=50/0

#NAME?

The formula contains a function name or cell reference Excel does not recognize.

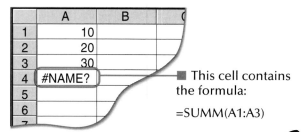

■ This cell contains the formula:

=SUMM(A1:A3)

In this example, the name of the SUM function was misspelled.

#REF!

The formula refers to a cell that is not valid.

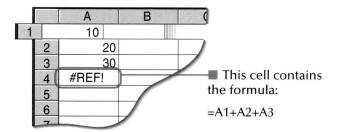

■ This cell contains the formula:

=A1+A2+A3

In this example, a row containing a cell used in the formula was deleted.

#VALUE!

The formula refers to a cell that Excel cannot use in a calculation.

	A	B	C
1	10		
2	20		
3	January		
4	#VALUE!		
5			
6			

■ This cell contains the formula:

=A1+A2+A3

In this example, a cell used in the formula contains text.

Circular Reference

A warning message appears when a formula refers to the cell containing the formula. This is called a circular reference.

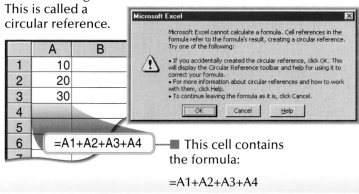

■ This cell contains the formula:

=A1+A2+A3+A4

COPY A FORMULA

> If you want to use the same formula several times in your worksheet, you can save time by copying the formula.

COPY A FORMULA—USING RELATIVE REFERENCES

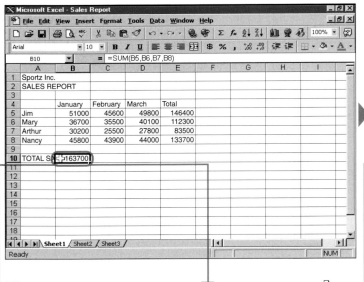

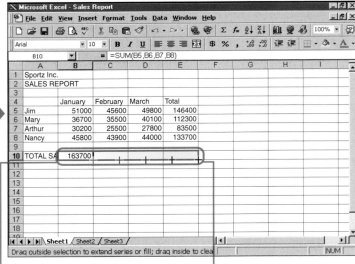

1 Enter the formula you want to copy to other cells.

■ In this example, cell **B10** contains the function **=SUM(B5,B6,B7,B8)**. A function is a ready-to-use formula.

2 Move the mouse ⊹ over the cell containing the formula you want to copy and then press the left mouse button.

3 Move the mouse ⊹ over the bottom right corner of the cell (⊹ changes to **+**).

4 Press and hold down the left mouse button as you move the mouse **+** over the cells you want to receive a copy of the formula. Then release the mouse button.

What is a relative reference?

A relative reference changes when you copy a formula.

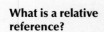

	A	B	C
1	10	20	5
2	20	30	10
3	30	40	20
4	60	90	35

=A1+A2+A3 → =B1+B2+B3   =C1+C2+C3

This cell contains the formula =A1+A2+A3.

If you copy the formula to other cells in your worksheet, Excel automatically changes the cell references in the new formulas.

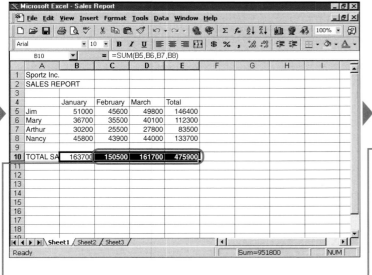

■ The results of the formulas appear.

■5 To see one of the new formulas, move the mouse ⊕ over a cell that received a copy of the formula and then press the left mouse button.

■ The formula bar displays the formula with the new cell references.

COPY A FORMULA

You can copy a formula to other cells in your worksheet to save time. If you do not want Excel to change a cell reference when you copy a formula, you can use an absolute reference.

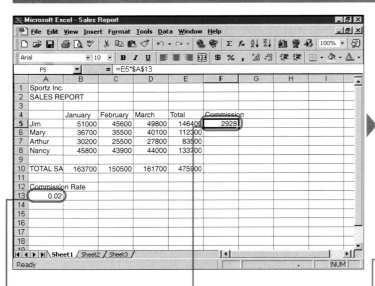

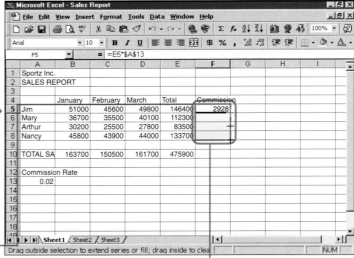

1 Enter the data you want to remain the same in all the formulas.

2 Enter the formula containing the absolute reference you want to copy to other cells. For information on absolute references, refer to the top of page 77.

■ In this example, cell **F5** contains the formula **=E5*$A$13**.

3 Move the mouse ⬚ over the cell containing the formula you want to copy and then press the left mouse button.

4 Move the mouse ⬚ over the bottom right corner of the cell (⬚ changes to ✛).

5 Press and hold down the left mouse button as you move the mouse ✛ over the cells you want to receive a copy of the formula. Then release the mouse button.

What is an absolute reference?

An absolute reference does not change when you copy a formula. To make a cell reference absolute, type a dollar sign ($) before both the column letter and row number (example: **$A$7**).

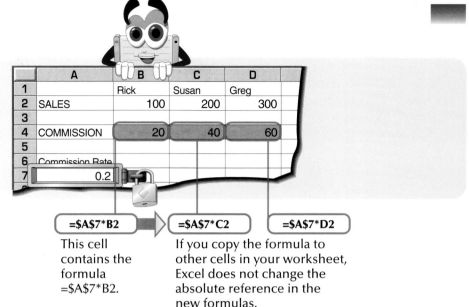

	A	B	C	D
1		Rick	Susan	Greg
2	SALES	100	200	300
3				
4	COMMISSION	20	40	60
5				
6	Commission Rate			
7	0.2			

=$A$7*B2 **=$A$7*C2** **=$A$7*D2**

This cell contains the formula =$A$7*B2.

If you copy the formula to other cells in your worksheet, Excel does not change the absolute reference in the new formulas.

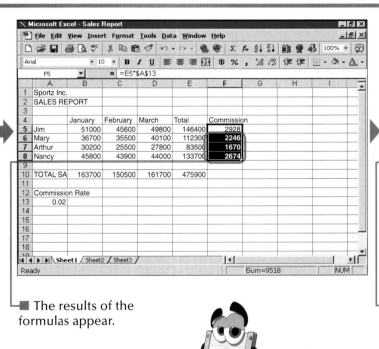

■ The results of the formulas appear.

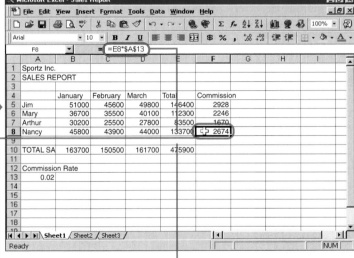

6 To see one of the new formulas, move the mouse ⬧ over a cell that received a copy of the formula and then press the left mouse button.

■ The absolute reference (example: **$A$13**) in the formula did not change.

■ The relative reference (example: **E8**) in the formula did change.

CHAPTER 5

CHANGE YOUR SCREEN DISPLAY

Are you interested in changing the way your worksheet appears on your screen? In this chapter you will learn how to display or hide a toolbar, zoom in or out and more.

ZOOM IN OR OUT

Excel lets you enlarge or reduce the display of data on your screen.

Changing the zoom setting will not affect the way data appears on a printed page.

ZOOM IN OR OUT

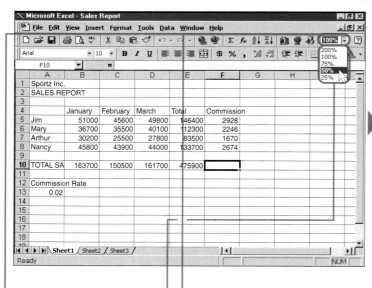

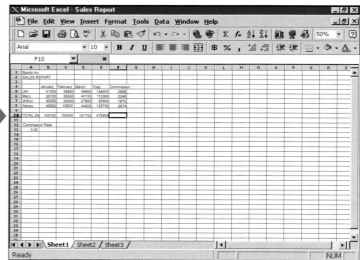

■ When you first start Excel, your worksheet appears in the 100% zoom setting.

1 To display a list of zoom settings, move the mouse ⌖ over ▾ in this area and then press the left mouse button.

2 Move the mouse ⌖ over the zoom setting you want to use and then press the left mouse button.

■ Your worksheet appears in the new zoom setting. You can edit your worksheet as usual.

■ To return to the normal zoom setting, repeat steps **1** and **2**, selecting **100%** in step **2**.

80

DISPLAY FULL SCREEN

You can display a larger working area by hiding parts of the Excel screen.

DISPLAY FULL SCREEN

1 Move the mouse over **View** and then press the left mouse button.

2 Move the mouse over **Full Screen** and then press the left mouse button.

■ Excel hides parts of the screen to display a larger working area.

■ To once again display the hidden parts of the screen, move the mouse over **Close Full Screen** and then press the left mouse button.

DISPLAY OR HIDE A TOOLBAR

Excel offers several toolbars that you can display or hide at any time. Each toolbar contains buttons that help you quickly perform common tasks.

DISPLAY OR HIDE A TOOLBAR

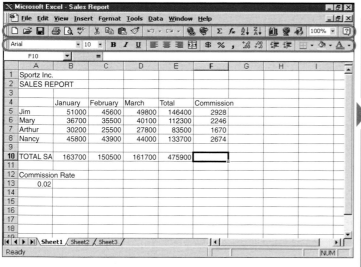

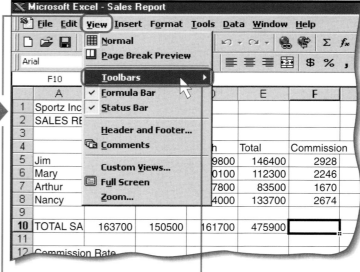

When you first start Excel, the Standard and Formatting toolbars appear on your screen.

Standard toolbar

Formatting toolbar

■1 To display or hide a toolbar, move the mouse ⊳ over **View** and then press the left mouse button.

■2 Move the mouse ⊳ over **Toolbars**.

Why would I hide a toolbar?

A screen displaying fewer toolbars provides a larger and less cluttered working area.

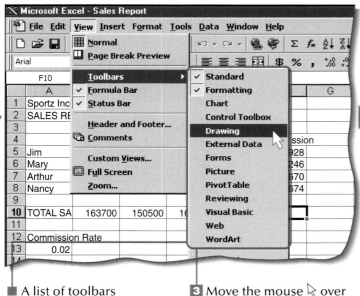

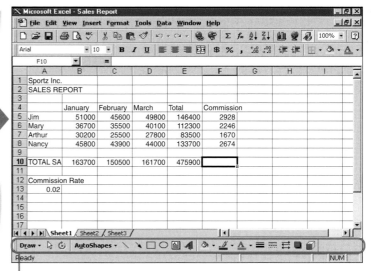

■ A list of toolbars appears. A check mark (✓) appears beside the name of each toolbar that is currently displayed.

3 Move the mouse ⌖ over the name of the toolbar you want to display or hide and then press the left mouse button.

■ Excel displays or hides the toolbar you selected.

FREEZE ROWS AND COLUMNS

You can freeze rows and columns in your worksheet so they will not move. This lets you keep headings on your screen as you move through a large worksheet.

FREEZE ROWS AND COLUMNS

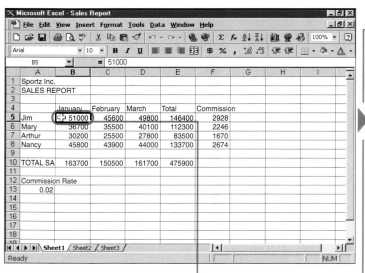

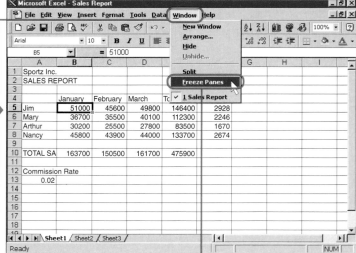

Excel will freeze the rows above and the columns to the left of the cell you select.

1 To select a cell, move the mouse ✛ over the cell and then press the left mouse button.

2 Move the mouse ▷ over **Window** and then press the left mouse button.

3 Move the mouse ▷ over **Freeze Panes** and then press the left mouse button.

How do I unfreeze rows and columns in my worksheet?

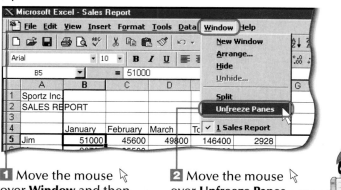

1 Move the mouse over **Window** and then press the left mouse button.

2 Move the mouse over **Unfreeze Panes** and then press the left mouse button.

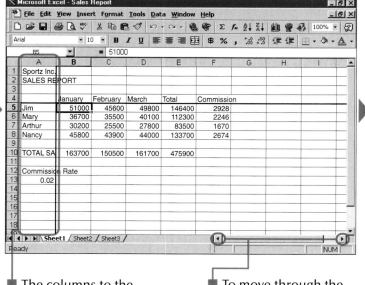

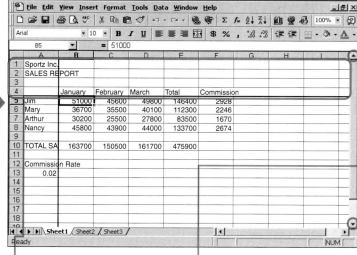

■ The columns to the left of the vertical line are frozen. These columns remain on your screen as you move through your worksheet.

■ To move through the columns to the right of the vertical line, move the mouse over ◀ or ▶ and then press the left mouse button.

■ The rows above the horizontal line are frozen. These rows remain on your screen as you move through your worksheet.

■ To move through the rows below the horizontal line, move the mouse over ▲ or ▼ and then press the left mouse button.

SPLIT A WORKSHEET

You can split your worksheet into separate sections. This lets you view different areas of a large worksheet at the same time.

SPLIT A WORKSHEET VERTICALLY

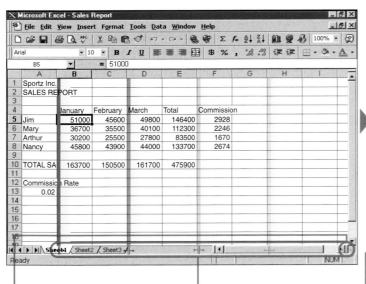

1 Move the mouse over this area (changes to ╫).

2 Press and hold down the left mouse button as you move the mouse ╫ to where you want to split your worksheet. Then release the mouse button.

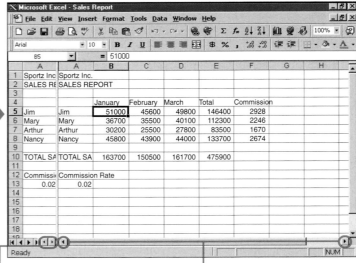

■ Your worksheet splits vertically into two sections.

■ To move through the columns to the left of the dividing line, move the mouse over ◄ or ► and then press the left mouse button.

■ To move through the columns to the right of the dividing line, move the mouse over ◄ or ► and then press the left mouse button.

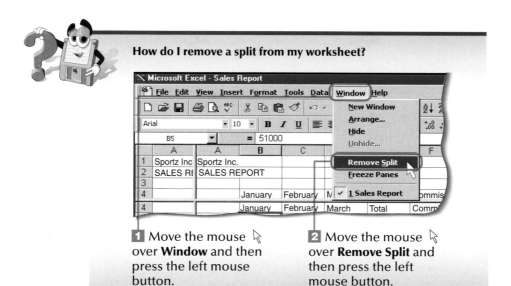

How do I remove a split from my worksheet?

1 Move the mouse over **Window** and then press the left mouse button.

2 Move the mouse over **Remove Split** and then press the left mouse button.

SPLIT A WORKSHEET HORIZONTALLY

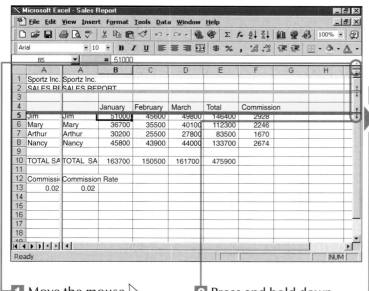

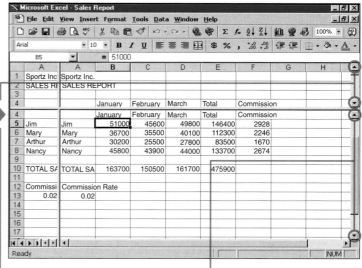

1 Move the mouse over this area (changes to ÷).

2 Press and hold down the left mouse button as you move the mouse ÷ to where you want to split your worksheet. Then release the mouse button.

■ Your worksheet splits horizontally into two sections.

■ To move through the rows above the dividing line, move the mouse over ▲ or ▼ and then press the left mouse button.

■ To move through the rows below the dividing line, move the mouse over ▲ or ▼ and then press the left mouse button.

	Jan	Feb	Mar	Total
East	7	7	5	19
West	6	4	7	17
South	8	7	9	24
Total	21	18	21	60

	Jan	Feb	Mar	Total
East	7	7	5	19
West	6	4	7	17
South	8	7	9	24
Total	21	18	21	60

	Jan		Feb	
East	$	7	$	7	$
West		6		4	
South		8		7	
Total	$	21	$	18	$

	Jan	Feb	Mar	Total
East	7	7	5	19
West	6	4	7	17
South	8	7	9	24
Total	21	18	21	60

CHAPTER 6

FORMAT YOUR WORKSHEETS

Are you wondering how to improve the appearance of your worksheet? This chapter shows you how to change fonts, align data, change cell and data colors, and much more.

CHANGE COLUMN WIDTH

You can improve the appearance of your worksheet and display hidden data by changing the width of columns.

FRUIT SALES

Fruit	Jan	Feb
Waterme	100	180
Apples	120	150
Bananas	200	220
Cherries	300	200
Strawberr	100	15
Mangoes	110	1

CHANGE COLUMN WIDTH

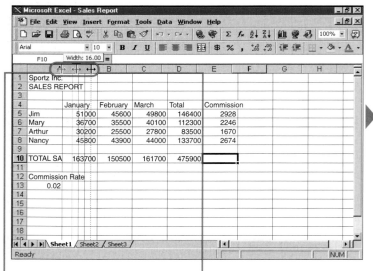

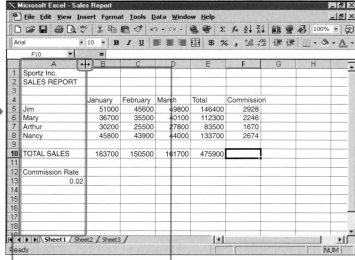

1 To change the width of a column, move the mouse ⬦ over the right edge of the column heading (⬦ changes to ↔).

2 Press and hold down the left mouse button as you move the column edge until the dotted line displays the column width you want. Then release the mouse button.

■ The column displays the new width.

FIT LONGEST ITEM

You can have Excel change a column width to fit the longest item in the column.

■ Move the mouse ⬦ over the right edge of the column heading (⬦ changes to ↔) and then quickly press the left mouse button twice.

CHANGE ROW HEIGHT

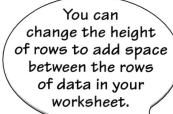

You can change the height of rows to add space between the rows of data in your worksheet.

FRUIT SALES

Fruit	Jan	Feb
Watermelons	100	180
Apples	120	150
Bananas	200	220
Cherries	300	200
Strawberries	100	150
Mangoes	110	110

CHANGE ROW HEIGHT

1 To change the height of a row, move the mouse ⊹ over the bottom edge of the row heading (⊹ changes to ‡).

2 Press and hold down the left mouse button as you move the row edge until the dotted line displays the row height you want. Then release the mouse button.

■ The row displays the new height.

FIT TALLEST ITEM

You can have Excel change a row height to fit the tallest item in the row.

■ Move the mouse ⊹ over the bottom edge of the row heading (⊹ changes to ‡) and then quickly press the left mouse button twice.

BOLD, ITALIC AND UNDERLINE

You can use the bold, italic and underline styles to emphasize data in your worksheet.

Bold   *Italic*   <u>Underline</u>

BOLD, ITALIC AND UNDERLINE

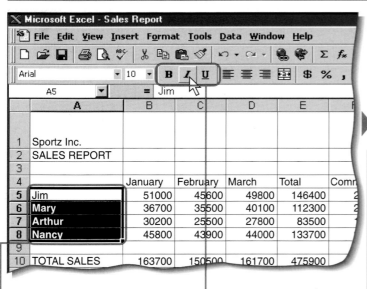

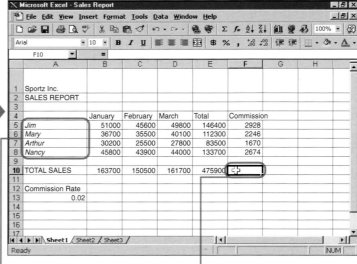

1 Select the cells containing the data you want to emphasize. To select cells, refer to page 16.

2 Move the mouse ↖ over one of the following options and then press the left mouse button.

B Bold
I Italic
<u>U</u> Underline

■ The data displays the style you selected.

■ To deselect cells, move the mouse ✛ over any cell and then press the left mouse button.

■ To remove a bold, italic or underline style, repeat steps **1** and **2**.

You can change the position of data in each cell of your worksheet.

CHANGE ALIGNMENT OF DATA

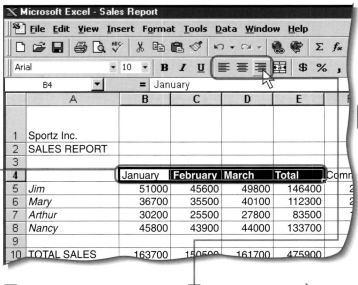

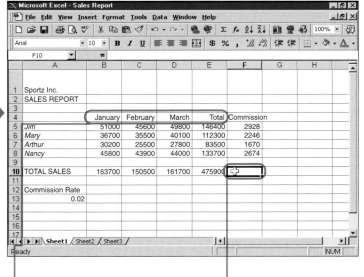

1 Select the cells containing the data you want to align differently. To select cells, refer to page 16.

2 Move the mouse ⫽ over one of the following options and then press the left mouse button.

▤ Left align

▤ Center

▤ Right align

■ Excel aligns the data.

■ To deselect cells, move the mouse ⊹ over any cell and then press the left mouse button.

CHANGE APPEARANCE OF NUMBERS

You can quickly change the appearance of numbers in your worksheet without retyping the numbers.

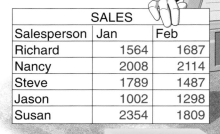

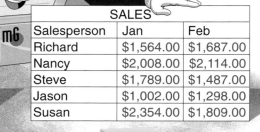

When you change the appearance of numbers, you do not change the value of the numbers.

CHANGE THE NUMBER STYLE

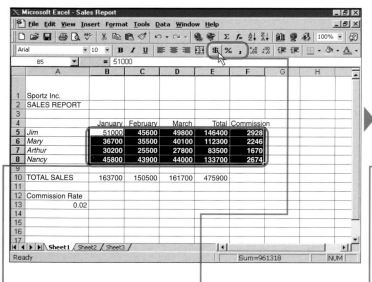

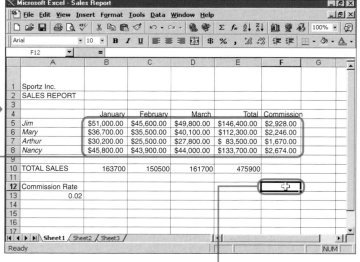

1 Select the cells containing the numbers you want to display in a different style. To select cells, refer to page 16.

2 Move the mouse over one of the following options and then press the left mouse button.

$ Currency style

% Percent style

, Comma style

■ The numbers display the style you selected.

■ To deselect cells, move the mouse over any cell and then press the left mouse button.

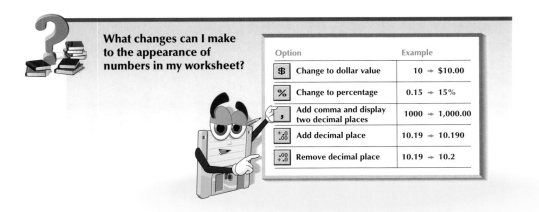

What changes can I make to the appearance of numbers in my worksheet?

Option		Example
$	Change to dollar value	10 → $10.00
%	Change to percentage	0.15 → 15%
,	Add comma and display two decimal places	1000 → 1,000.00
+.0 .00	Add decimal place	10.19 → 10.190
.00 +.0	Remove decimal place	10.19 → 10.2

ADD OR REMOVE A DECIMAL PLACE

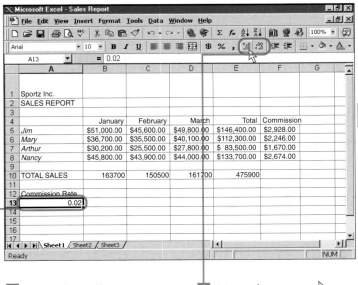

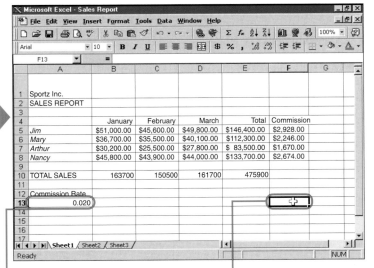

1 Select the cells containing the numbers you want to change. To select cells, refer to page 16.

2 Move the mouse ⬚ over one of the following options and then press the left mouse button.

⬚ Add decimal place

⬚ Remove decimal place

■ The numbers display the number of decimal places you selected.

■ To deselect cells, move the mouse ⬚ over any cell and then press the left mouse button.

CHANGE APPEARANCE OF NUMBERS

Excel offers many different ways that you can display the numbers in your worksheet to make them easier to read.

Currency

$1,000
$1,000.00
($1,000)

Date

4-Mar-97
Mar-97
03/04/97
March 4, 1997

Scientific

3.456E+03
3.E+03

When you change the appearance of numbers, you do not change the value of the numbers.

CHANGE APPEARANCE OF NUMBERS

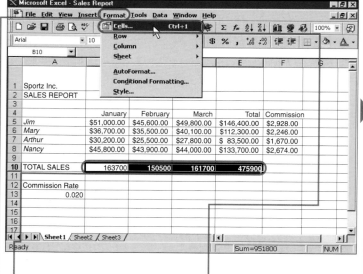

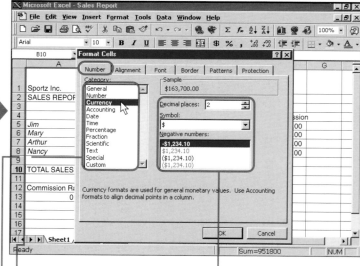

1 Select the cells containing the numbers you want to display differently. To select cells, refer to page 16.

2 Move the mouse ⌖ over **Format** and then press the left mouse button.

3 Move the mouse ⌖ over **Cells** and then press the left mouse button.

■ The **Format Cells** dialog box appears.

4 Move the mouse ⌖ over the **Number** tab and then press the left mouse button.

5 Move the mouse ⌖ over the category that identifies the numbers in your worksheet and then press the left mouse button.

■ This area displays all the options for the category you selected. Each category displays a different set of options.

Why did number signs (#) appear in a cell after I changed the appearance of numbers?

If number signs (#) appear in a cell, the column is not wide enough to display the entire number. To change the column width, refer to page 90.

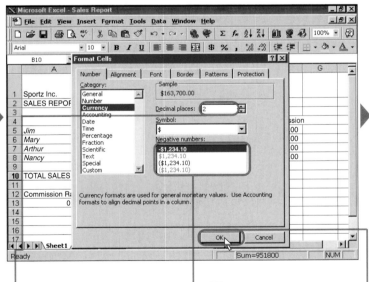

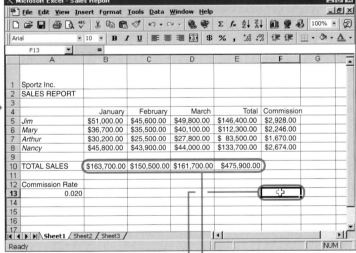

6 To select the number of decimal places you want the numbers to display, move the mouse I over this area and then quickly press the left mouse button twice. Then type the number of decimal places.

7 To select the way you want negative numbers to appear, move the mouse over one of the available styles and then press the left mouse button.

8 To apply the changes, move the mouse over **OK** and then press the left mouse button.

■ The numbers display the changes.

■ To deselect cells, move the mouse over any cell and then press the left mouse button.

CHANGE FONT OF DATA

You can enhance the appearance of data in your worksheet by changing the font.

CHANGE FONT OF DATA

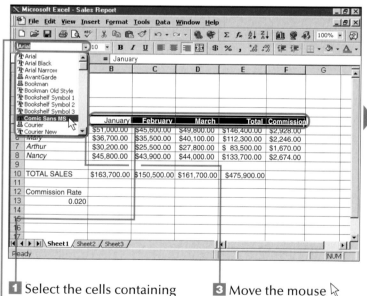

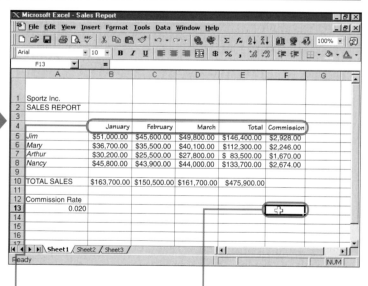

1 Select the cells containing the data you want to change to a new font. To select cells, refer to page 16.

2 To display a list of the available fonts, move the mouse ⌀ over ▾ in this area and then press the left mouse button.

3 Move the mouse ⌀ over the font you want to use and then press the left mouse button.

■ The data displays the font you selected.

■ To deselect cells, move the mouse ⬧ over any cell and then press the left mouse button.

CHANGE SIZE OF DATA

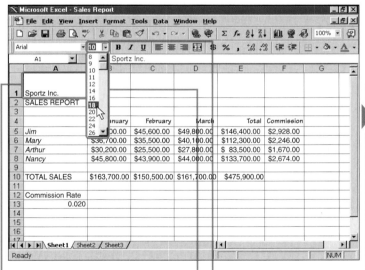 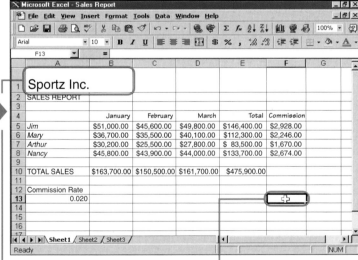

1 Select the cells containing the data you want to change to a new size. To select cells, refer to page 16.

2 To display a list of the available sizes, move the mouse ⌖ over ▾ in this area and then press the left mouse button.

3 Move the mouse ⌖ over the size you want to use and then press the left mouse button.

■ The data displays the size you selected.

■ To deselect cells, move the mouse ⌖ over any cell and then press the left mouse button.

99

CHANGE FONT OF DATA

You can change the design, style and size of data in your worksheet at the same time.

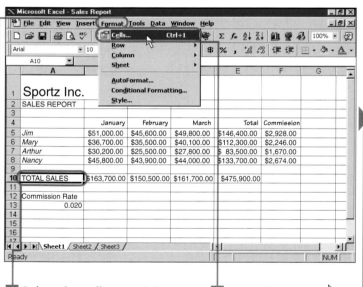

CHANGE FONT OF DATA

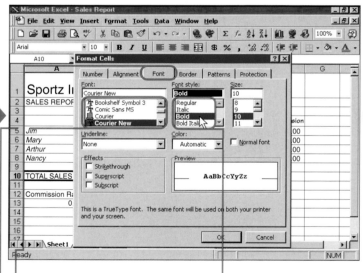

1 Select the cells containing the data you want to display differently. To select cells, refer to page 16.

2 Move the mouse over **Format** and then press the left mouse button.

3 Move the mouse over **Cells** and then press the left mouse button.

■ The **Format Cells** dialog box appears.

4 Move the mouse over the **Font** tab and then press the left mouse button.

5 To change the design of the data, move the mouse over the font you want to use and then press the left mouse button.

6 To change the style of the data, move the mouse over the style you want to use and then press the left mouse button.

What determines which fonts are available on my computer?

The fonts available on your computer may be different from the fonts on other computers. The available fonts depend on your printer and the setup of your computer.

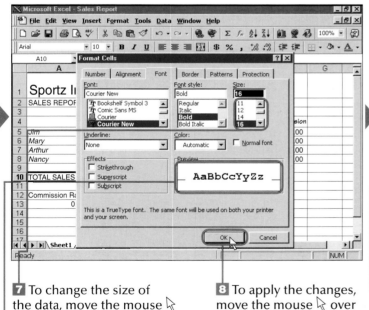

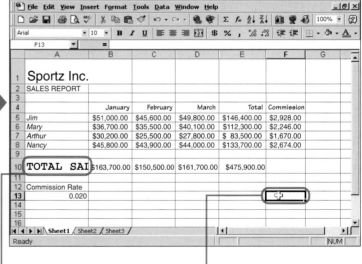

7 To change the size of the data, move the mouse over the size you want to use and then press the left mouse button.

■ This area displays a preview of all the options you selected.

8 To apply the changes, move the mouse over **OK** and then press the left mouse button.

■ The data displays the changes.

■ To deselect cells, move the mouse over any cell and then press the left mouse button.

INDENT DATA

You can use the Indent feature to move data away from the left edge of a cell.

INDENT DATA

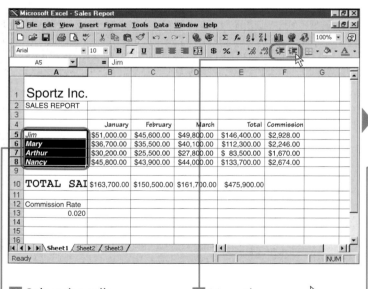

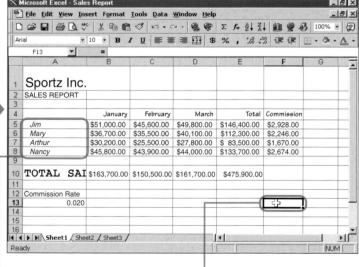

1 Select the cells containing the data you want to indent. To select cells, refer to page 16.

2 Move the mouse ⇖ over one of the following options and then press the left mouse button.

   Move data to the left

   Move data to the right

■ Excel indents the data.

■ To deselect cells, move the mouse ⇩ over any cell and then press the left mouse button.

> You can center data across several columns in your worksheet. This is useful for centering titles over your data.

CENTER DATA ACROSS COLUMNS

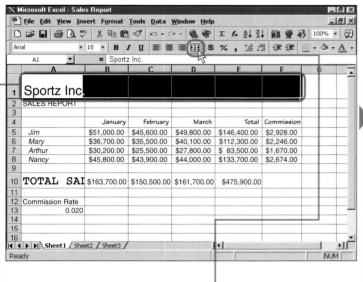

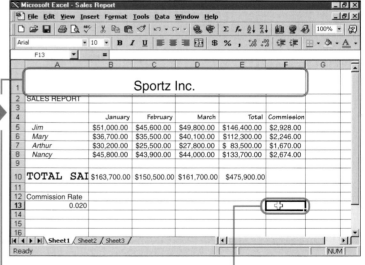

1 Select the cells you want to center the data across. To select cells, refer to page 16.

Note: The first cell you select should contain the data you want to center.

2 Move the mouse over 🖻 and then press the left mouse button.

■ Excel centers the data across the cells you selected.

■ To deselect cells, move the mouse ⊕ over any cell and then press the left mouse button.

You can display long lines of text within cells by wrapping the text.

WRAP TEXT IN CELLS

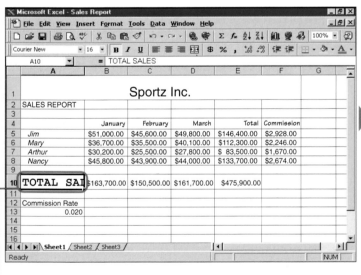

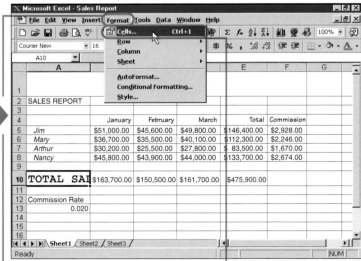

1 Select the cells containing the text you want to wrap. To select cells, refer to page 16.

2 Move the mouse ⬚ over **Format** and then press the left mouse button.

3 Move the mouse ⬚ over **Cells** and then press the left mouse button.

■ The **Format Cells** dialog box appears.

Can I wrap text as I type?

When you want to start a new line of text as you type, press and hold down Alt and then press Enter on your keyboard. Then release both keys.

>Click<

>Click<

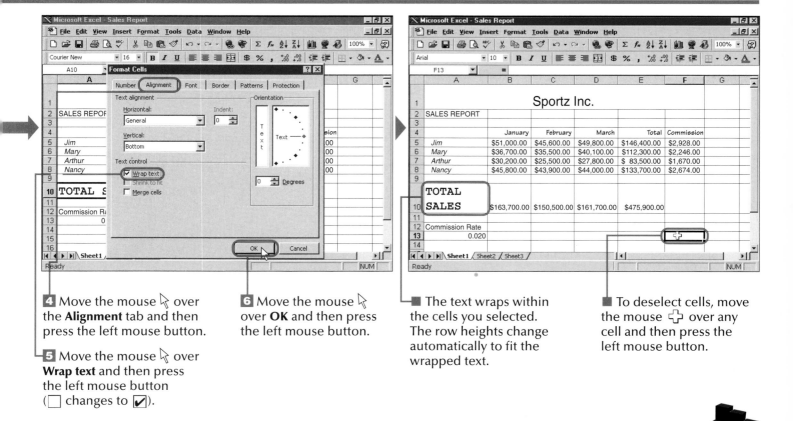

4 Move the mouse ⃝ over the **Alignment** tab and then press the left mouse button.

5 Move the mouse ⃝ over **Wrap text** and then press the left mouse button (☐ changes to ☑).

6 Move the mouse ⃝ over **OK** and then press the left mouse button.

■ The text wraps within the cells you selected. The row heights change automatically to fit the wrapped text.

■ To deselect cells, move the mouse ⊹ over any cell and then press the left mouse button.

ROTATE DATA IN CELLS

You can easily rotate data within cells in your worksheet. This helps you emphasize row and column headings.

ROTATE DATA IN CELLS

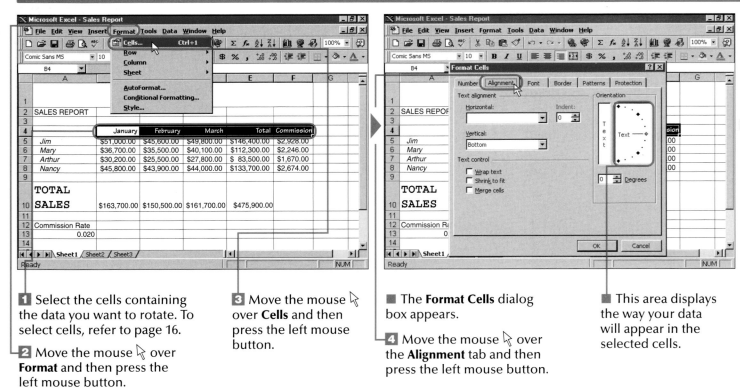

■1 Select the cells containing the data you want to rotate. To select cells, refer to page 16.

■2 Move the mouse ⍟ over **Format** and then press the left mouse button.

■3 Move the mouse ⍟ over **Cells** and then press the left mouse button.

■ The **Format Cells** dialog box appears.

■4 Move the mouse ⍟ over the **Alignment** tab and then press the left mouse button.

■ This area displays the way your data will appear in the selected cells.

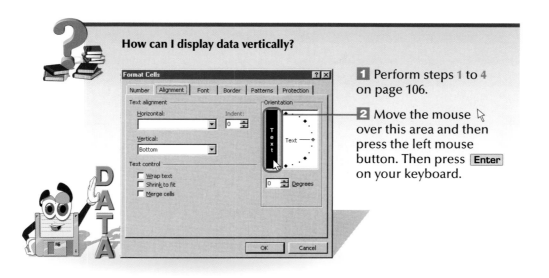

How can I display data vertically?

1 Perform steps 1 to 4 on page 106.

2 Move the mouse over this area and then press the left mouse button. Then press Enter on your keyboard.

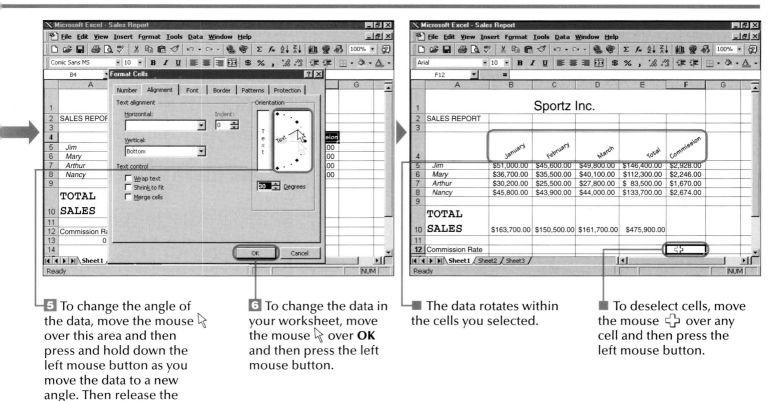

5 To change the angle of the data, move the mouse over this area and then press and hold down the left mouse button as you move the data to a new angle. Then release the mouse button.

6 To change the data in your worksheet, move the mouse over **OK** and then press the left mouse button.

■ The data rotates within the cells you selected.

■ To deselect cells, move the mouse over any cell and then press the left mouse button.

ADD BORDERS

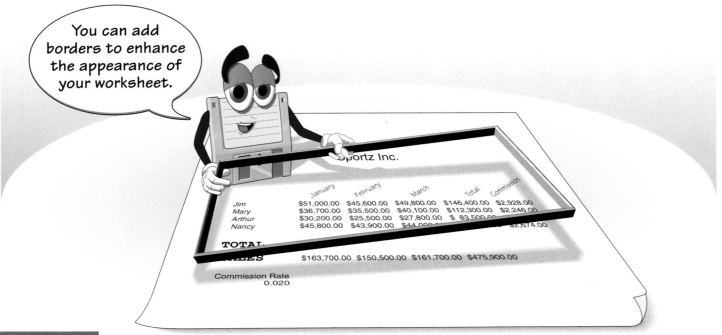

You can add borders to enhance the appearance of your worksheet.

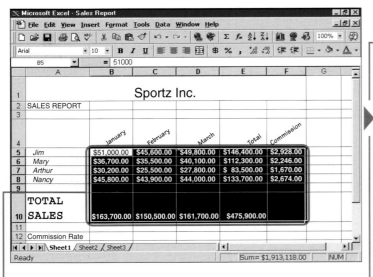

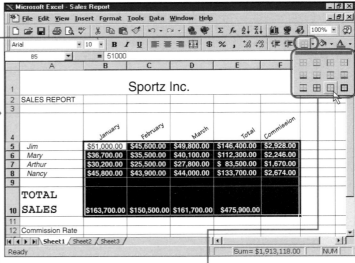

1 Select the cells you want to display borders. To select cells, refer to page 16.

2 Move the mouse over ▾ in this area and then press the left mouse button.

3 Move the mouse over the type of border you want to add and then press the left mouse button.

Can I print lines in my worksheet without adding borders?

Instead of adding borders to your worksheet, you can have Excel automatically print light lines, called gridlines, around each cell. To print gridlines, refer to page 128.

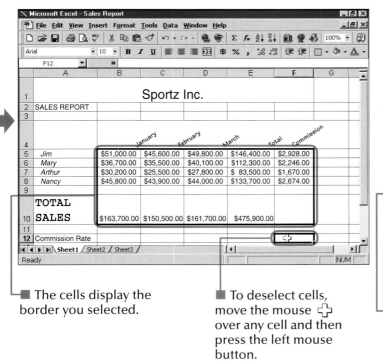

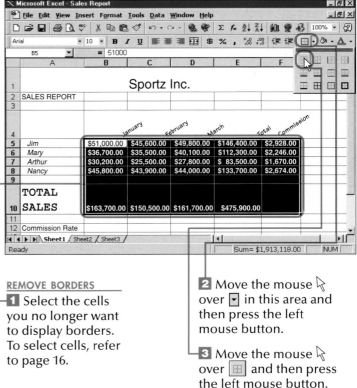

■ The cells display the border you selected.

■ To deselect cells, move the mouse ✛ over any cell and then press the left mouse button.

REMOVE BORDERS

1 Select the cells you no longer want to display borders. To select cells, refer to page 16.

2 Move the mouse ⌖ over ▾ in this area and then press the left mouse button.

3 Move the mouse ⌖ over ⊞ and then press the left mouse button.

CHANGE COLOR

You can make your worksheet more attractive by adding color.

CHANGE CELL COLOR

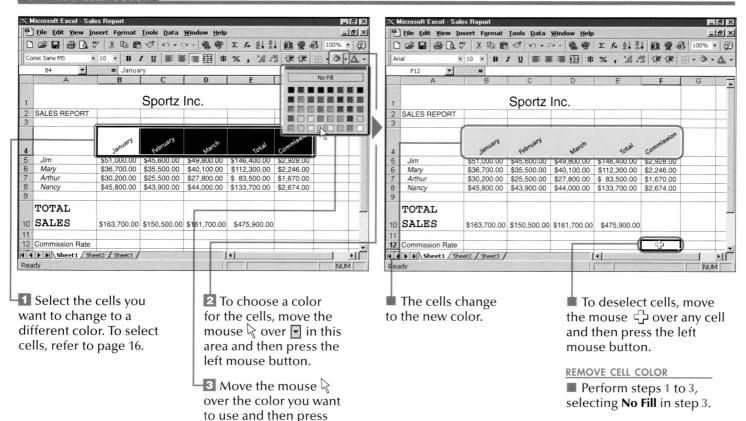

1 Select the cells you want to change to a different color. To select cells, refer to page 16.

2 To choose a color for the cells, move the mouse ⌖ over ▼ in this area and then press the left mouse button.

3 Move the mouse ⌖ over the color you want to use and then press the left mouse button.

■ The cells change to the new color.

■ To deselect cells, move the mouse ⌖ over any cell and then press the left mouse button.

REMOVE CELL COLOR

■ Perform steps **1** to **3**, selecting **No Fill** in step **3**.

What colors should I choose?

When adding color to your worksheet, make sure you choose cell and data colors that work well together. For example, red text on a blue background is difficult to read. To choose from many ready-to-use designs offered by Excel, refer to page 116.

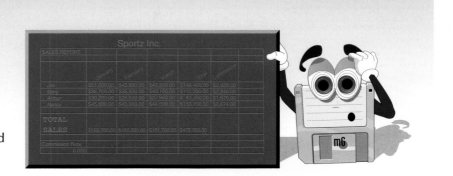

CHANGE DATA COLOR

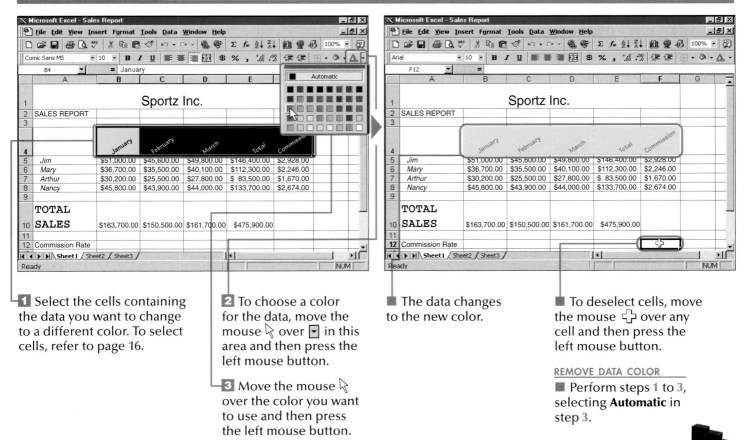

1 Select the cells containing the data you want to change to a different color. To select cells, refer to page 16.

2 To choose a color for the data, move the mouse ⬚ over ▾ in this area and then press the left mouse button.

3 Move the mouse ⬚ over the color you want to use and then press the left mouse button.

■ The data changes to the new color.

■ To deselect cells, move the mouse ⬚ over any cell and then press the left mouse button.

REMOVE DATA COLOR

■ Perform steps **1** to **3**, selecting **Automatic** in step **3**.

111

COPY FORMATTING

If you like the appearance of a cell in your worksheet, you can make other cells look exactly the same.

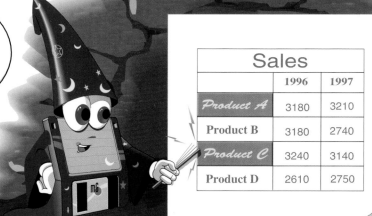

Sales		
	1996	**1997**
Product A	3180	3210
Product B	3180	2740
Product C	3240	3140
Product D	2610	2750

COPY FORMATTING

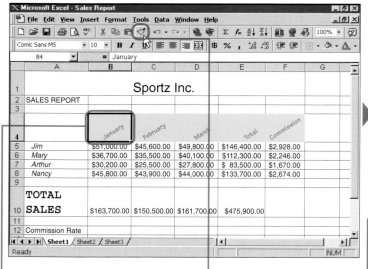

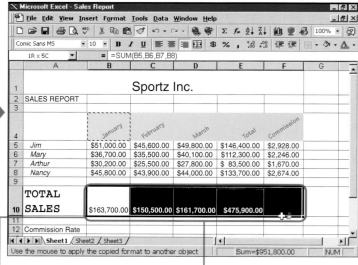

1 Move the mouse ✛ over a cell displaying the formatting you want to copy to other cells and then press the left mouse button.

2 Move the mouse ↖ over 🖌 and then press the left mouse button.

■ The mouse ↖ changes to ✛🖌 when over your worksheet.

3 Select the cells you want to display the same formatting. To select cells, refer to page 16.

You can copy formatting to several locations in your worksheet at once.

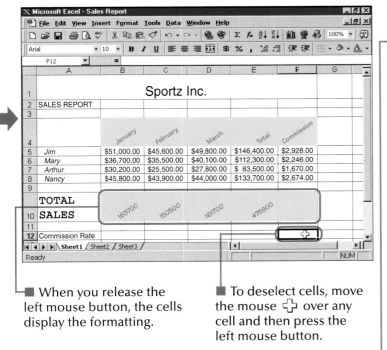

■ When you release the left mouse button, the cells display the formatting.

■ To deselect cells, move the mouse ⊕ over any cell and then press the left mouse button.

1 Move the mouse ⊕ over a cell displaying the formatting you want to copy to other cells and then press the left mouse button.

2 Move the mouse ⊕ over 🖌 and then quickly press the left mouse button twice.

3 Select the cells you want to display the same formatting. Repeat this step until you have selected all the cells you want to display the formatting.

4 Move the mouse ⊕ over 🖌 and then press the left mouse button.

You can easily remove all the formatting from cells in your worksheet.

CLEAR FORMATTING

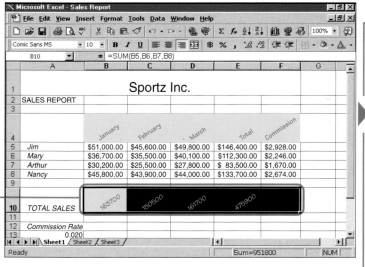

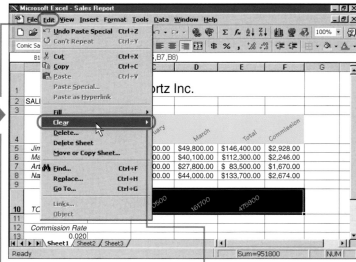

1 Select the cells containing the formatting you want to remove. To select cells, refer to page 16.

2 Move the mouse over **Edit** and then press the left mouse button.

3 Move the mouse over **Clear**.

How can I keep the formatting but remove the data from cells?

To keep the formatting but remove the data from cells, select the cells containing the data you want to remove. Then press Delete on your keyboard.

Miles Traveled		
Salesperson	Jan	Feb
Richard	15 1	1687.08
Nancy	d	2114.73
Steve	9.67	1487.09
Jason	002.08	12 8.56
Susa	235	67

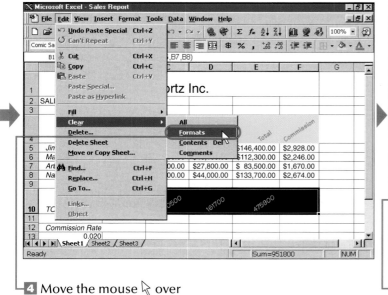

4 Move the mouse ⌖ over **Formats** and then press the left mouse button.

■ All the formatting disappears from the cells you selected.

■ To deselect cells, move the mouse ⌖ over any cell and then press the left mouse button.

115

QUICKLY APPLY A DESIGN

Excel offers many ready-to-use designs you can choose from to give your worksheet a new appearance.

QUICKLY APPLY A DESIGN

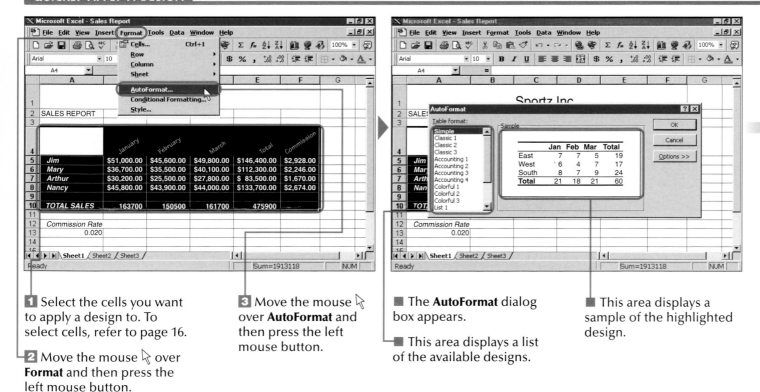

1 Select the cells you want to apply a design to. To select cells, refer to page 16.

2 Move the mouse ⍦ over **Format** and then press the left mouse button.

3 Move the mouse ⍦ over **AutoFormat** and then press the left mouse button.

■ The **AutoFormat** dialog box appears.

■ This area displays a list of the available designs.

■ This area displays a sample of the highlighted design.

116

What are some designs offered by Excel?

	Jan	Feb	Mar	Total
East	7	7	5	19
West	6	4	7	17
South	8	7	9	24
Total	21	18	21	60

List 2

	Jan	Feb	Mar	Total
East	$ 7	$ 7	$ 5	$ 19
West	6	4	7	17
South	8	7	9	24
Total	$ 21	$ 18	$ 21	$ 60

Accounting 2

	Jan	Feb	Mar	Total
East	7	7	5	19
West	6	4	7	17
South	8	7	9	24
Total	21	18	21	60

Colorful 1

	Jan	Feb	Mar	Total
East	7	7	5	19
West	6	4	7	17
South	8	7	9	24
Total	21	18	21	60

3D Effects 1

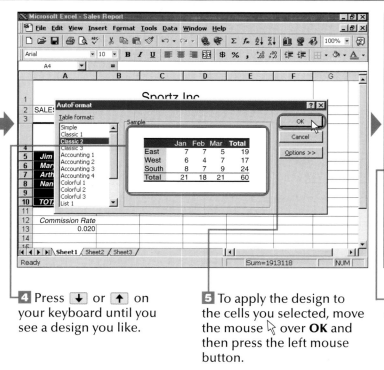

4 Press ⬇ or ⬆ on your keyboard until you see a design you like.

5 To apply the design to the cells you selected, move the mouse ⬚ over **OK** and then press the left mouse button.

■ The cells display the design you selected.

■ To deselect cells, move the mouse ⬚ over any cell and then press the left mouse button.

REMOVE AUTOFORMAT

■ Perform steps **1** to **5**, selecting **None** in step **4**.

CHAPTER 7

PRINT YOUR WORKSHEETS

Are you ready to print your worksheet?
In this chapter you will learn how to print
your worksheet and change the way your
worksheet appears on a printed page.

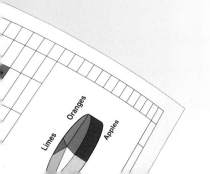

PREVIEW A WORKSHEET

You can see on your screen how your worksheet will look when printed.

PREVIEW A WORKSHEET

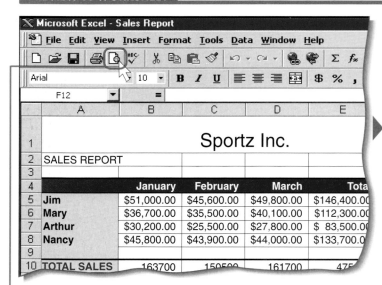

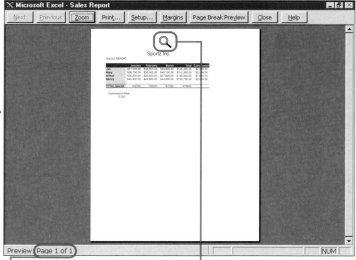

1 Move the mouse ⌕ over 🔍 and then press the left mouse button.

■ The Print Preview window appears.

■ This area tells you which page is displayed and the total number of pages in your worksheet.

Note: If you have a black-and-white printer, Excel displays the page in black and white.

2 To magnify an area of the page, move the mouse ⌕ over the area (⌕ changes to 🔍) and then press the left mouse button.

What should I do before printing my worksheet?

Before printing your worksheet, preview the worksheet to ensure it will print the way you want. Also make sure your printer is turned on and contains paper.

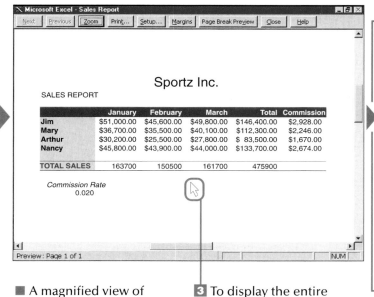

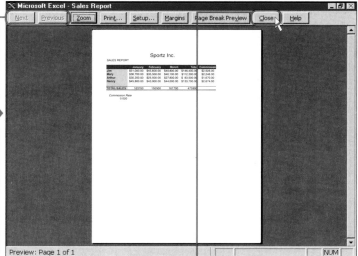

■ A magnified view of the area appears.

3 To display the entire page again, move the mouse ↖ anywhere over the page and then press the left mouse button.

■ If your worksheet contains more than one page, move the mouse ↖ over one of these options and then press the left mouse button to view the next or previous page.

4 To close the Print Preview window, move the mouse ↖ over **Close** and then press the left mouse button.

PRINT A WORKSHEET

You can produce a paper copy of the worksheet displayed on your screen.

PRINT A WORKSHEET

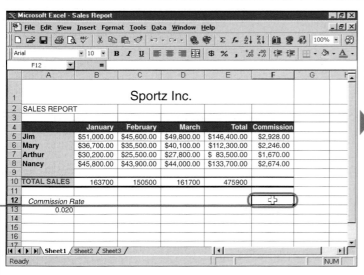

1 To print a worksheet, move the mouse ✛ over any cell in the worksheet and then press the left mouse button.

■ To print only part of the worksheet, select the cells you want to print. To select cells, refer to page 16.

2 Move the mouse ⌖ over **File** and then press the left mouse button.

3 Move the mouse ⌖ over **Print** and then press the left mouse button.

■ The **Print** dialog box appears.

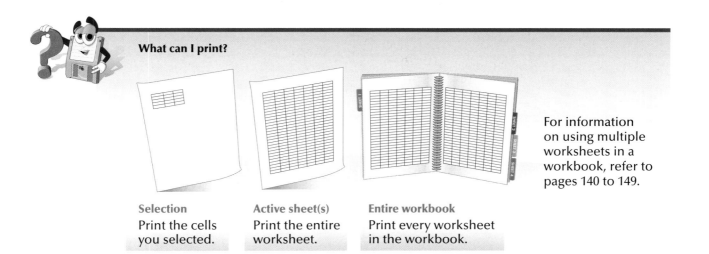

What can I print?

For information on using multiple worksheets in a workbook, refer to pages 140 to 149.

Selection
Print the cells you selected.

Active sheet(s)
Print the entire worksheet.

Entire workbook
Print every worksheet in the workbook.

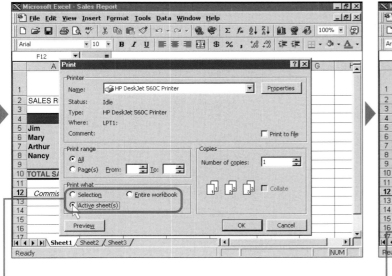

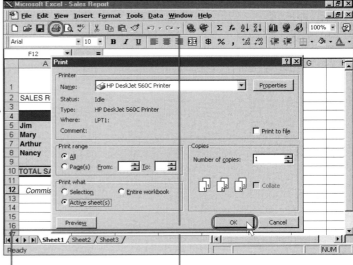

4 Move the mouse ☐ over what you want to print and then press the left mouse button (○ changes to ◉).

Note: For information on what you can print, refer to the top of this page.

5 Move the mouse ☐ over **OK** and then press the left mouse button.

QUICKLY PRINT ENTIRE WORKSHEET

■ To quickly print the worksheet displayed on your screen, move the mouse ☐ over 🖨 and then press the left mouse button.

123

CHANGE MARGINS

A margin is the amount of space between data and an edge of your paper. You can easily change the margins.

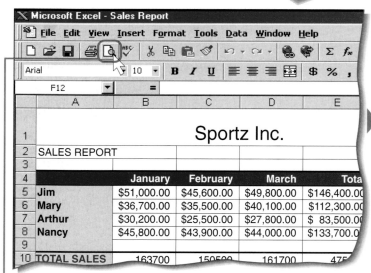

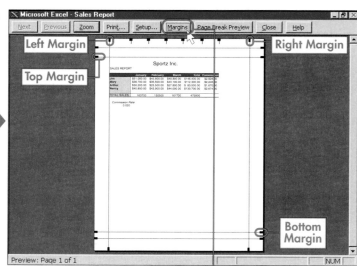

1 To display your worksheet in the Print Preview window, move the mouse ⟍ over 🔍 and then press the left mouse button.

■ Your worksheet appears in the Print Preview window. For information on previewing a worksheet, refer to page 120.

2 If the margins are not displayed, move the mouse ⟍ over **Margins** and then press the left mouse button.

124

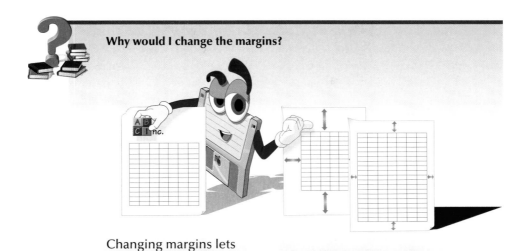

Why would I change the margins?

Changing margins lets you accommodate letterhead and other specialty paper.

You can also change the margins to fit more or less information on a page.

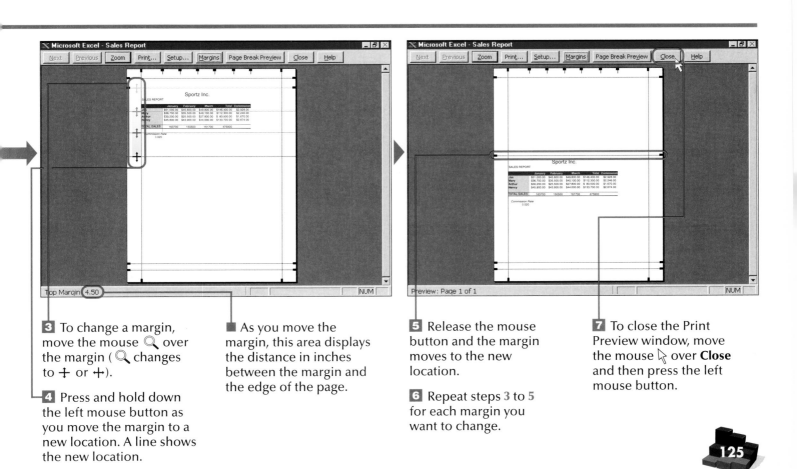

3 To change a margin, move the mouse ⌕ over the margin (⌕ changes to ✛ or ➕).

4 Press and hold down the left mouse button as you move the margin to a new location. A line shows the new location.

■ As you move the margin, this area displays the distance in inches between the margin and the edge of the page.

5 Release the mouse button and the margin moves to the new location.

6 Repeat steps **3** to **5** for each margin you want to change.

7 To close the Print Preview window, move the mouse ⍓ over **Close** and then press the left mouse button.

CENTER DATA ON A PAGE

You can center data horizontally and vertically between the margins on a page.

CENTER DATA ON A PAGE

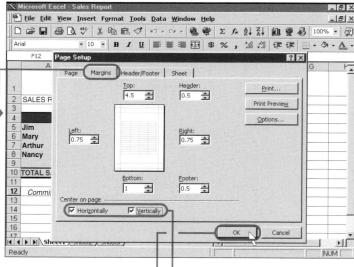

1 Move the mouse ⟶ over **File** and then press the left mouse button.

2 Move the mouse ⟶ over **Page Setup** and then press the left mouse button.

■ The **Page Setup** dialog box appears.

3 Move the mouse ⟶ over the **Margins** tab and then press the left mouse button.

4 Move the mouse ⟶ over the way you want to center the data and then press the left mouse button (☐ changes to ☑). You can select both center options if you wish.

5 Move the mouse ⟶ over **OK** and then press the left mouse button.

You can change the orientation of your printed worksheet.

PORTRAIT

LANDSCAPE

The landscape orientation is ideal if you want a wide worksheet to fit on one page.

CHANGE PAGE ORIENTATION

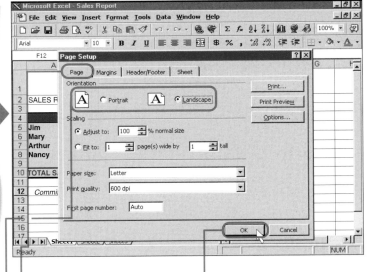

1 Move the mouse over **File** and then press the left mouse button.

2 Move the mouse over **Page Setup** and then press the left mouse button.

■ The **Page Setup** dialog box appears.

3 Move the mouse over the **Page** tab and then press the left mouse button.

4 Move the mouse over the orientation you want to use and then press the left mouse button (○ changes to ◉).

5 Move the mouse over **OK** and then press the left mouse button.

CHANGE PRINT OPTIONS

You can change the way your worksheet appears on a printed page.

CHANGE PRINT OPTIONS

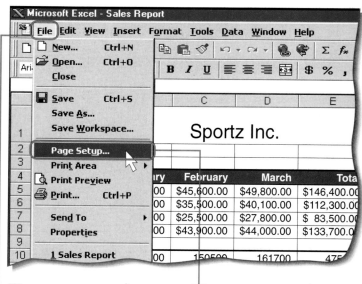

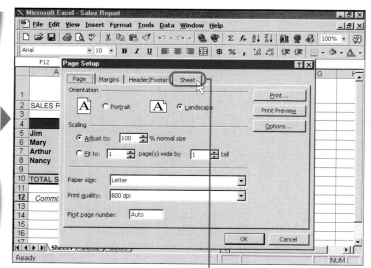

1 Move the mouse ▷ over **File** and then press the left mouse button.

2 Move the mouse ▷ over **Page Setup** and then press the left mouse button.

■ The **Page Setup** dialog box appears.

3 Move the mouse ▷ over the **Sheet** tab and then press the left mouse button.

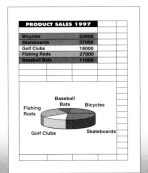

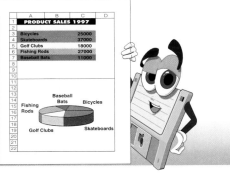

Gridlines

Prints lines around each cell in your worksheet.

Black and white

Prints your worksheet in black and white. This can make a colored worksheet printed on a black-and-white printer easier to read.

Draft quality

Does not print gridlines or most graphics to reduce printing time.

Row and column headings

Prints the row numbers and column letters.

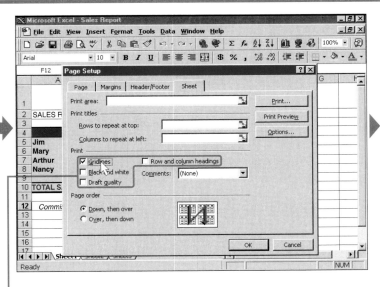

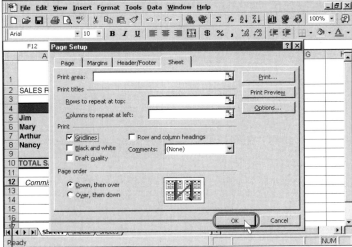

■4 Move the mouse ⮕ over the print option you want to select and then press the left mouse button (☐ changes to ✔).

Note: For information on the print options, refer to the top of this page.

■5 Repeat step 4 for each print option you want to select.

■6 Move the mouse ⮕ over **OK** and then press the left mouse button.

■ The print options you selected only change the way your worksheet appears on a printed page. The print options do not affect the way your worksheet appears on your screen.

If you want to start a new page at a specific place in your worksheet, you can add a page break. A page break defines where one page ends and another begins.

When you fill a page with data, Excel automatically starts a new page by inserting a page break for you.

INSERT A PAGE BREAK

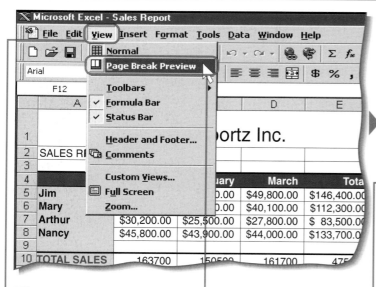

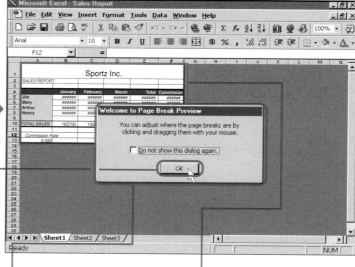

1 To display the page breaks in your worksheet, move the mouse ⌖ over **View** and then press the left mouse button.

2 Move the mouse ⌖ over **Page Break Preview** and then press the left mouse button.

■ A **Welcome** dialog box appears.

3 To close the dialog box, move the mouse ⌖ over **OK** and then press the left mouse button.

■ Blue lines show where page breaks currently occur in your worksheet.

Note: To return to the normal view at any time, repeat steps 1 and 2, selecting Normal in step 2.

How can I move a page break?

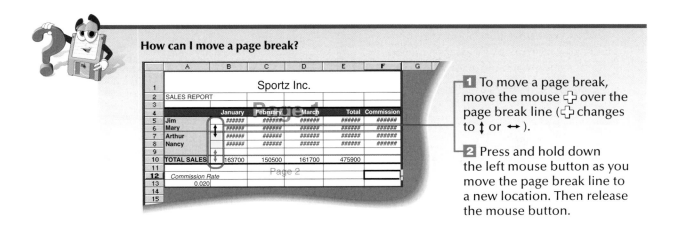

1 To move a page break, move the mouse ✛ over the page break line (✛ changes to ↕ or ↔).

2 Press and hold down the left mouse button as you move the page break line to a new location. Then release the mouse button.

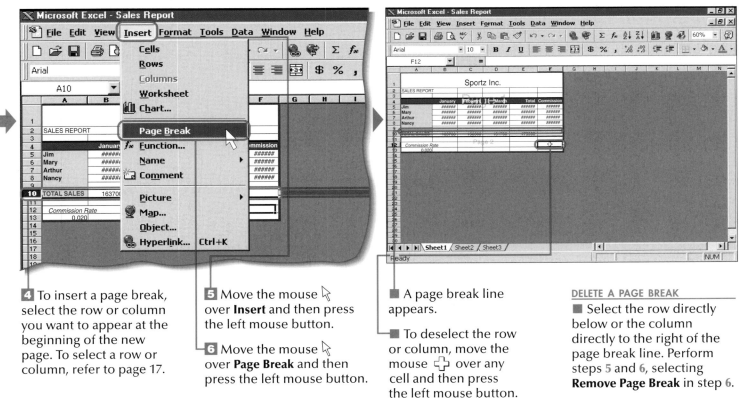

4 To insert a page break, select the row or column you want to appear at the beginning of the new page. To select a row or column, refer to page 17.

5 Move the mouse ▷ over **Insert** and then press the left mouse button.

6 Move the mouse ▷ over **Page Break** and then press the left mouse button.

■ A page break line appears.

■ To deselect the row or column, move the mouse ✛ over any cell and then press the left mouse button.

DELETE A PAGE BREAK

■ Select the row directly below or the column directly to the right of the page break line. Perform steps **5** and **6**, selecting **Remove Page Break** in step **6**.

ADD A HEADER OR FOOTER

Headers and footers appear at the top and bottom of each printed page.

Sales Report ← Header

Page 1 ← Footer

ADD A HEADER OR FOOTER

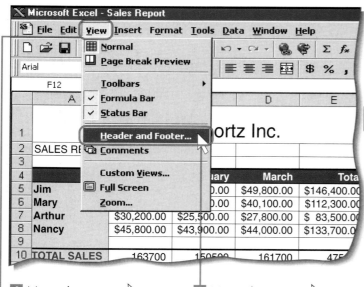

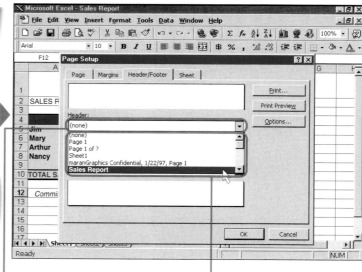

1 Move the mouse ⊹ over **View** and then press the left mouse button.

2 Move the mouse ⊹ over **Header and Footer** and then press the left mouse button.

■ The **Page Setup** dialog box appears.

3 To view a list of headers you can use, move the mouse ⊹ over this area and then press the left mouse button.

4 Move the mouse ⊹ over the header you want to use and then press the left mouse button.

132

How can I see what a header or footer will look like before I print my worksheet?

You can use the Print Preview feature to view a header or footer before you print your worksheet. To use the Print Preview feature, refer to page 120.

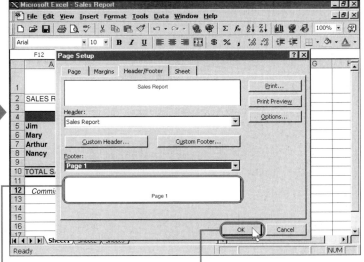

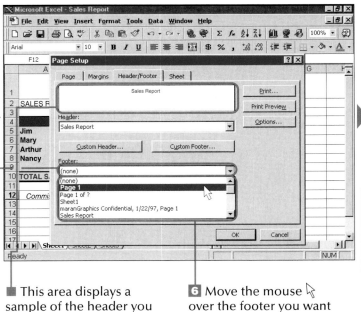

■ This area displays a sample of the header you selected.

5 To view a list of footers you can use, move the mouse ⇧ over this area and then press the left mouse button.

6 Move the mouse ⇧ over the footer you want to use and then press the left mouse button.

■ This area displays a sample of the footer you selected.

7 To add the header and footer to your worksheet, move the mouse ⇧ over **OK** and then press the left mouse button.

CHANGE SIZE OF PRINTED DATA

You can reduce the size of printed data to print your worksheet on a specific number of pages.

This feature is useful when the last page of your worksheet contains a small amount of data that you want to fit on the second-last page.

CHANGE SIZE OF PRINTED DATA

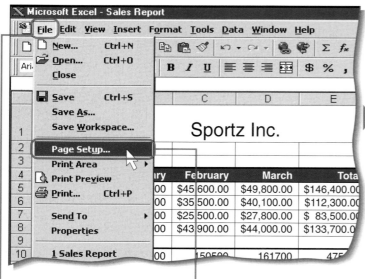

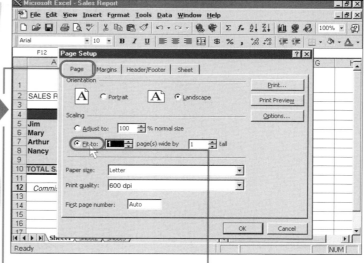

1 Move the mouse over **File** and then press the left mouse button.

2 Move the mouse over **Page Setup** and then press the left mouse button.

■ The **Page Setup** dialog box appears.

3 Move the mouse over the **Page** tab and then press the left mouse button.

4 Move the mouse over **Fit to** and then press the left mouse button (O changes to ●).

When I change the size of my printed data, what information does Excel require?

When you change the size of your printed data, you need to tell Excel how many pages you want the data to print across and down.

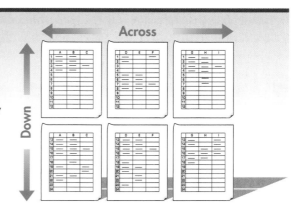

MANUALLY CHANGE SIZE OF PRINTED DATA

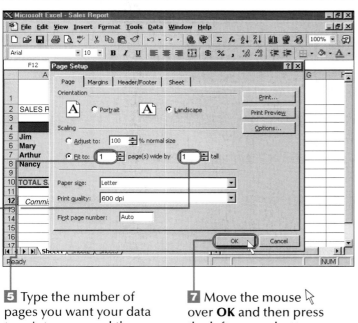

5 Type the number of pages you want your data to print across and then press **Tab** on your keyboard.

6 Type the number of pages you want your data to print down.

7 Move the mouse ⌖ over **OK** and then press the left mouse button.

■ Excel will change the size of the printed data to fit on the number of pages you specified.

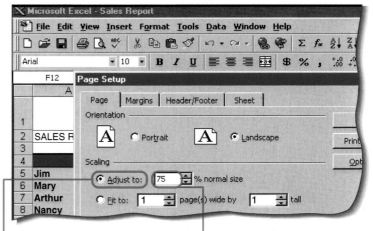

You can manually reduce or enlarge the size of printed data.

1 Perform steps **1** to **3** on page 134.

2 Move the mouse ⌖ over **Adjust to** and then press the left mouse button (O changes to ◉).

3 Type the percentage you want to use and then press **Enter** on your keyboard.

Note: A percentage over 100 will increase the size of the printed data. A percentage under 100 will decrease the size of the printed data.

REPEAT TITLES ON PRINTED PAGES

You can display the same rows or columns of titles on every printed page. This helps you review worksheets that print on more than one page.

REPEAT TITLES ON PRINTED PAGES

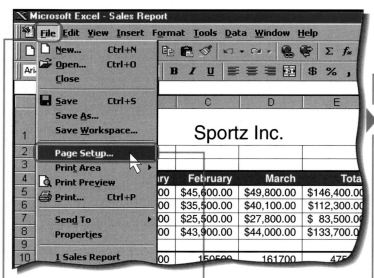

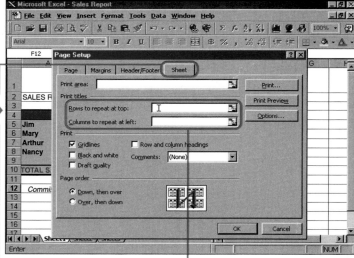

1 Move the mouse ⟍ over **File** and then press the left mouse button.

2 Move the mouse ⟍ over **Page Setup** and then press the left mouse button.

■ The **Page Setup** dialog box appears.

3 Move the mouse ⟍ over the **Sheet** tab and then press the left mouse button.

4 Move the mouse I over the box beside one of the following options and then press the left mouse button.

Rows to repeat at top
Repeat titles across the top of each page.

Columns to repeat at left
Repeat titles down the left side of each page.

136

How can I see what the repeated titles will look like before I print my worksheet?

You can use the Print Preview feature to view the repeated titles before you print your worksheet. To use the Print Preview feature, refer to page 120.

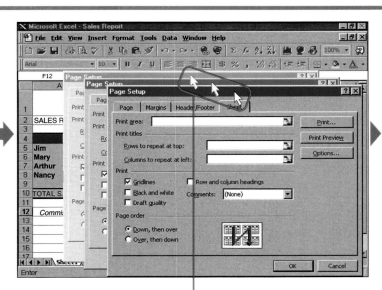

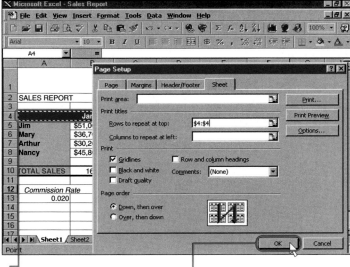

■ If the dialog box covers the rows or columns containing the titles you want to repeat, you can move the dialog box to a new location.

5 To move the dialog box, move the mouse over the title bar.

6 Press and hold down the left mouse button as you move the dialog box to a new location. Then release the mouse button.

7 Select one cell in each row or column containing the titles you want to repeat. To select cells, refer to page 16.

8 Move the mouse over **OK** and then press the left mouse button.

CHAPTER 8

WORK WITH MULTIPLE WORKSHEETS

Would you like to work with more than one worksheet at a time? This chapter teaches you how.

SWITCH BETWEEN WORKSHEETS

The worksheet displayed on your screen is one of several worksheets in your workbook. You can easily switch between the worksheets.

SWITCH BETWEEN WORKSHEETS

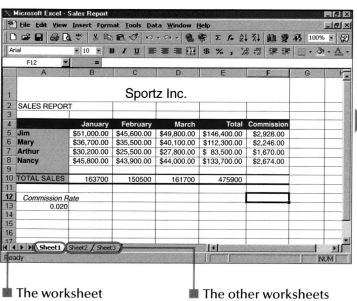

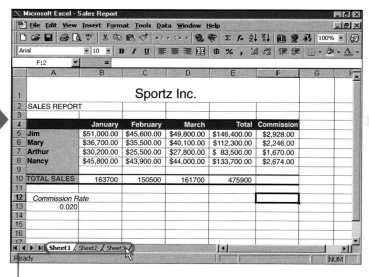

■ The worksheet displayed on your screen has a white tab.

■ The other worksheets in the workbook have gray tabs. The contents of these worksheets are hidden.

1 To display the contents of a worksheet, move the mouse ⍾ over the tab of the worksheet and then press the left mouse button.

Why would I need more than one worksheet?

Worksheets allow you to keep related information in a single file, called a workbook. For example, information for each division of a company can be stored on a separate worksheet in one workbook.

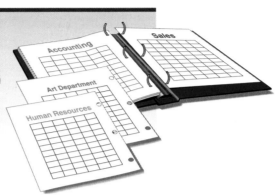

BROWSE THROUGH TABS

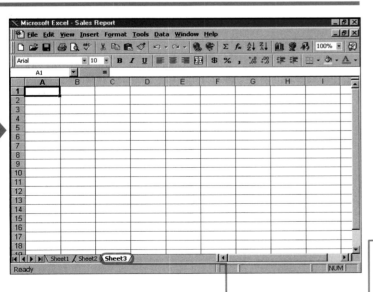

■ The contents of the worksheet appear. The contents of the other worksheets in the workbook are hidden.

■ The worksheet you selected now has a white tab.

■ If you have many worksheets in your workbook, you may not be able to see all the tabs.

Note: To insert additional worksheets, refer to page 142.

1 To browse through the tabs, move the mouse ⌖ over one of the following options and then press the left mouse button.

|◀| Display first tab
|◀| Display tab to the left
|▶| Display tab to the right
|▶| Display last tab

INSERT A WORKSHEET

You can easily insert a new worksheet to add related information to a workbook.

INSERT A WORKSHEET

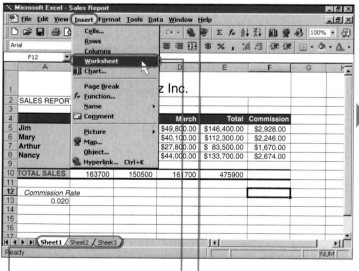

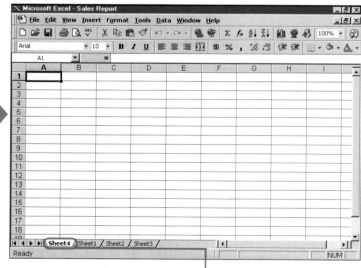

1 Move the mouse over the tab of the worksheet you want to appear after the new worksheet and then press the left mouse button.

2 Move the mouse over **Insert** and then press the left mouse button.

3 Move the mouse over **Worksheet** and then press the left mouse button.

■ The new worksheet appears.

■ Excel displays a tab for the new worksheet.

DELETE A WORKSHEET

You can permanently remove a worksheet you no longer need.

DELETE A WORKSHEET

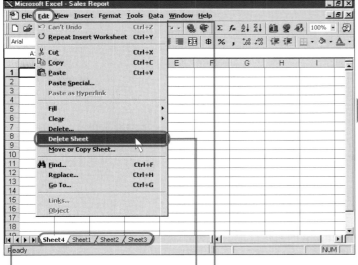

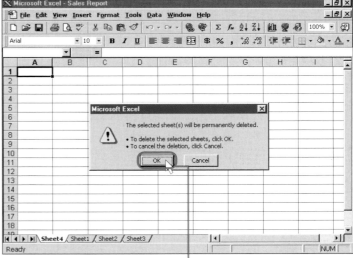

1 Move the mouse over the tab of the worksheet you want to delete and then press the left mouse button.

2 Move the mouse over **Edit** and then press the left mouse button.

3 Move the mouse over **Delete Sheet** and then press the left mouse button.

■ A warning dialog box appears.

4 To permanently delete the worksheet, move the mouse over **OK** and then press the left mouse button.

RENAME A WORKSHEET

You can give each worksheet in a workbook a descriptive name. This helps you remember where you stored your data.

Income Expenses Revenue

RENAME A WORKSHEET

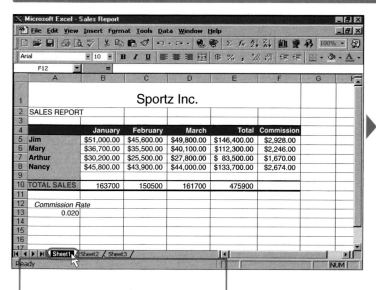

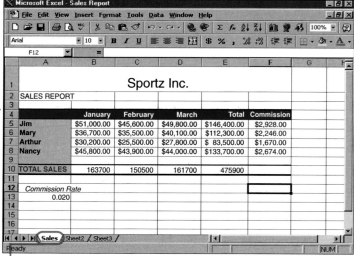

1 Move the mouse ⌖ over the tab of the worksheet you want to rename and then quickly press the left mouse button twice.

■ The current name is highlighted.

2 Type a new name and then press **Enter** on your keyboard. A worksheet name can contain up to 31 characters, including spaces.

MOVE A WORKSHEET

You can reorganize information by moving a worksheet to a new location in a workbook.

MOVE A WORKSHEET

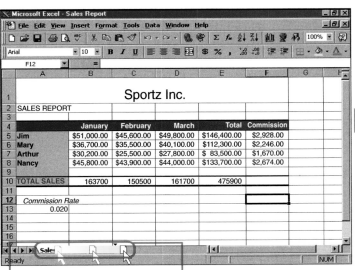

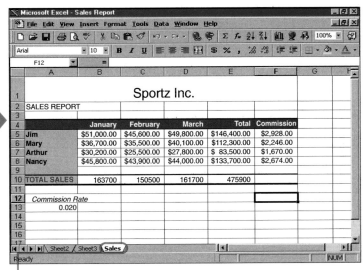

1 Move the mouse ⌖ over the tab of the worksheet you want to move.

2 Press and hold down the left mouse button as you move the worksheet to a new location.

■ An arrow (▾) shows where the worksheet will appear.

3 Release the mouse button and the worksheet appears in the new location.

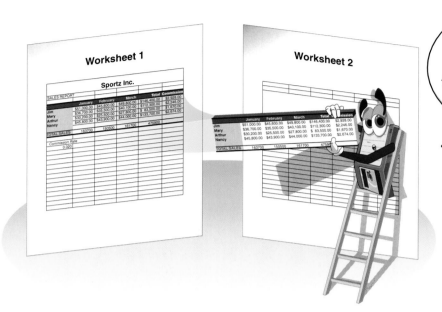

You can copy or move data from one worksheet to another. This will save you time when you want to use data from another worksheet.

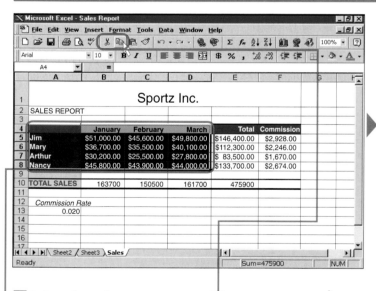

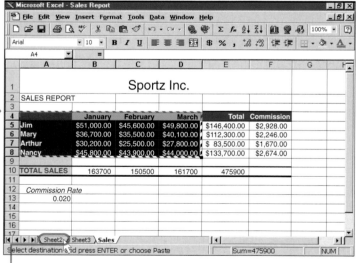

1 Select the cells containing the data you want to place in another worksheet. To select cells, refer to page 16.

2 Move the mouse ⌖ over one of the following options and then press the left mouse button.

✂ Move the data

▤ Copy the data

3 Move the mouse ⌖ over the tab of the worksheet where you want to place the data and then press the left mouse button.

Note: To place the data in another workbook, open the workbook and then perform step 3. To open a workbook, refer to page 32.

What is the difference between copying and moving data?

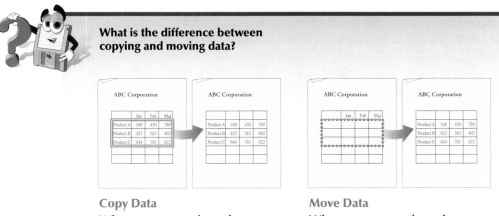

Copy Data
When you copy data, the original data remains in its place.

Move Data
When you move data, the original data disappears.

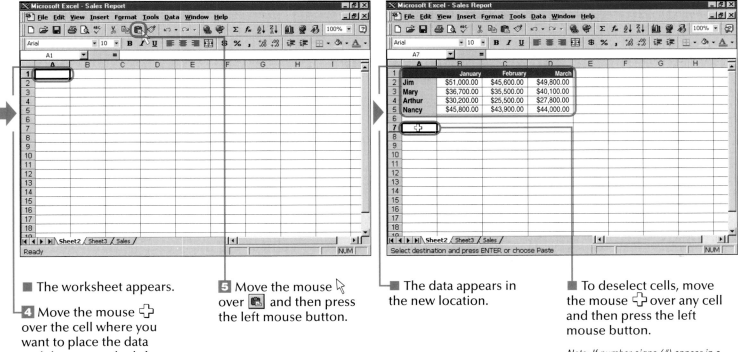

■ The worksheet appears.

4 Move the mouse ⊹ over the cell where you want to place the data and then press the left mouse button. This cell will become the top left cell of the new location.

5 Move the mouse ⊳ over 📋 and then press the left mouse button.

■ The data appears in the new location.

■ To deselect cells, move the mouse ⊹ over any cell and then press the left mouse button.

Note: If number signs (#) appear in a cell, the column is too narrow to fit the data. To change the column width, refer to page 90.

ENTER A FORMULA ACROSS WORKSHEETS

> You can enter a formula in one worksheet that uses data from other worksheets.

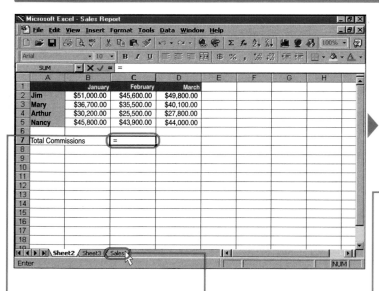

ENTER A FORMULA ACROSS WORKSHEETS

1 Move the mouse ⊹ over the cell where you want to enter a formula and then press the left mouse button.

2 Type an equal sign (=) to begin the formula.

3 Move the mouse ⟍ over the tab of a worksheet containing data you want to use in the formula and then press the left mouse button.

■ The worksheet appears.

4 Move the mouse ⊹ over a cell containing data you want to use in the formula and then press the left mouse button.

5 Type an operator (example: *).

What happens if I change a number used in a formula?

If you change a number used in a formula, Excel will automatically calculate a new result. This ensures that your calculations are always up-to-date.

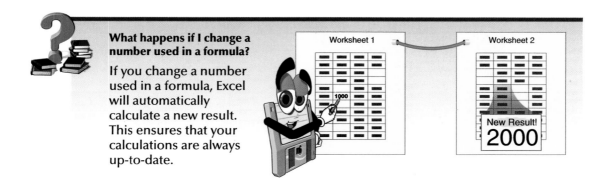

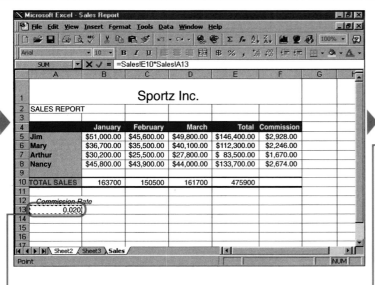

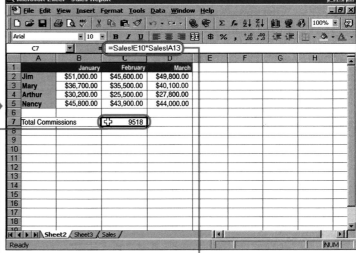

6 Repeat steps **3** to **5** until you have selected all the cells containing data you want to use in the formula.

*Note: In this example, cells **E10** and **A13** are multiplied together.*

7 Press **Enter** on your keyboard to complete the formula.

■ The result of the calculation appears in the cell you selected in step **1**.

8 To view the formula you entered, move the mouse ⊕ over the cell containing the formula and then press the left mouse button.

■ The formula bar displays the worksheet name and the cell reference for each cell used in the formula.

CHAPTER 9

WORK WITH CHARTS

Do you want to visually display your worksheet data in a chart? In this chapter you will learn how to create, change and print charts.

INTRODUCTION TO CHARTS

A chart allows you to visually display your worksheet data. Excel offers many different chart types.

Data Series

A group of related data representing one row or column from your worksheet. Each data series is a specific color, pattern or symbol.

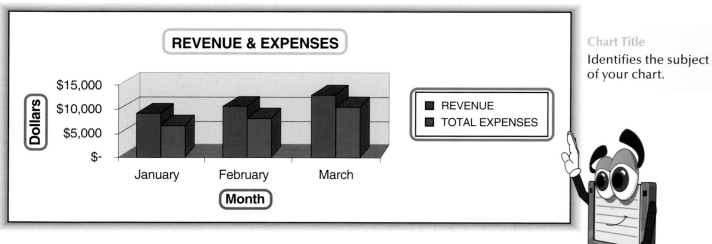

Chart Title

Identifies the subject of your chart.

Y-Axis Title
Indicates the unit of measure used in your chart.

X-Axis Title
Indicates the categories used in your chart.

Legend
Identifies the color, pattern or symbol used for each data series in your chart.

COMMON CHART TYPES

Area

An area chart is useful for showing the amount of change in data over time. Each line represents a data series.

Line

A line chart is useful for showing changes to data at regular intervals. Each line represents a data series.

Bar

A bar chart is useful for comparing individual items. Each bar represents an item in a data series.

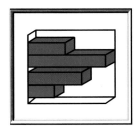

Pie

A pie chart is useful for showing the relationship of parts to a whole. Each piece of a pie represents an item in a data series. A pie chart can show only one data series at a time.

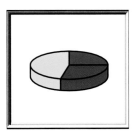

Column

A column chart is useful for showing changes to data over time or comparing individual items. Each bar represents an item in a data series.

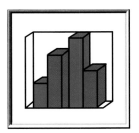

Radar

A radar chart is useful for comparing the items in several data series. Each data series is shown as a line around a central point.

Doughnut

A doughnut chart is useful for showing the relationship of parts to a whole. Unlike a pie chart, a doughnut chart can display more than one data series. Each ring represents a data series.

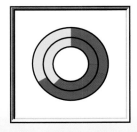

XY (Scatter)

An xy (scatter) chart is useful for showing the relationship between two or more data series measured at uneven intervals.

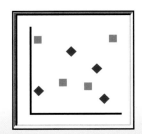

CREATE A CHART

You can create a chart to graphically display your worksheet data.

Sportz Inc.

	March	Total	Commission
	$800.00	$146,400.00	$2,928.00
	$40,100.00	$112,300.00	$2,246.00
	$00.00	$27,800.00	$ 83,500.00	$1,670.00
Nancy	$43,900.00	$44,000.00	$133,700.00	$2,674.00
TOTAL SALES	163700	150500	161700	475900

Commission Rate

CREATE A CHART

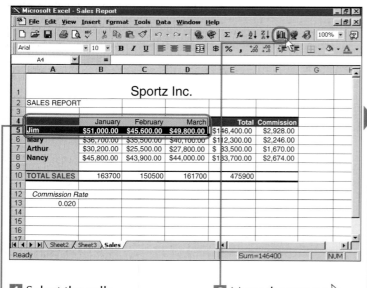

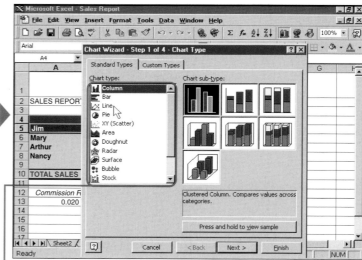

1 Select the cells containing the data you want to display in a chart, including the row and column labels. To select cells, refer to page 16.

2 Move the mouse ⌖ over 📊 and then press the left mouse button.

■ The **Chart Wizard** dialog box appears.

3 Move the mouse ⌖ over the type of chart you want to create and then press the left mouse button.

Note: After you create a chart, you can easily change the type of chart. For information, refer to page 158.

Can I change my selections?

While creating a chart, you can return to a previous step at any time to change the choices you made.

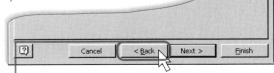

■ To return to the previous step, move the mouse ℟ over **Back** and then press the left mouse button.

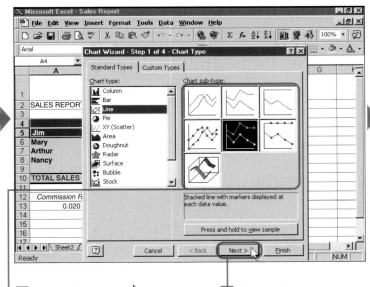

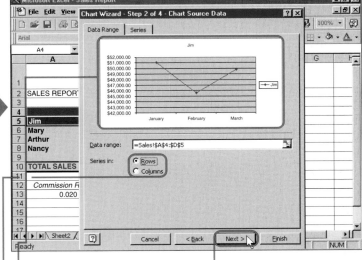

4 Move the mouse ℟ over the chart design you want to use and then press the left mouse button.

Note: The available designs depend on the type of chart you selected in step 3.

5 To continue, move the mouse ℟ over **Next** and then press the left mouse button.

■ This area displays a sample of the chart.

6 To select the way you want Excel to plot the data from your worksheet, move the mouse ℟ over one of these options and then press the left mouse button (○ changes to ◉).

7 To continue, move the mouse ℟ over **Next** and then press the left mouse button.

CONT⚙NUED➡

You can add titles to your chart to make the chart easier to understand.

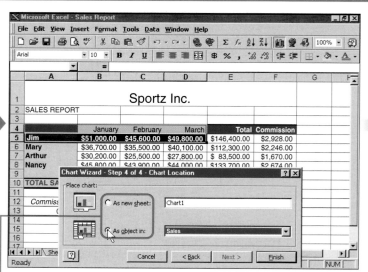

CREATE A CHART (CONTINUED)

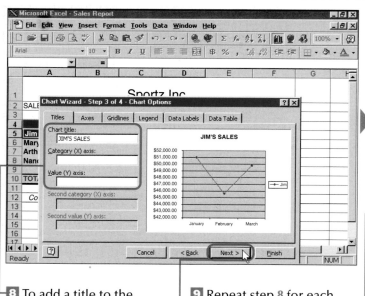

8 To add a title to the chart, move the mouse I over the box for the title you want to add and then press the left mouse button. Then type the title.

9 Repeat step **8** for each title you want to add.

10 To continue, move the mouse ⇧ over **Next** and then press the left mouse button.

11 To choose where you want to display the chart, move the mouse ⇧ over one of these options and then press the left mouse button (○ changes to ⊙).

As new sheet

Display chart on its own sheet, called a chart sheet.

As object in

Display chart on the same worksheet as the data.

What happens if I change data used in a chart?

If you change data used in a chart, Excel will automatically update the chart.

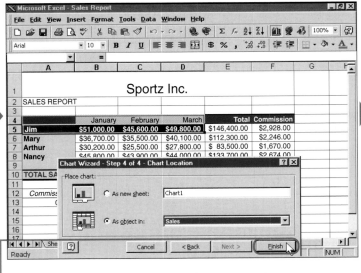

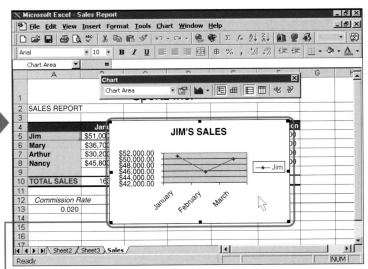

12 To complete the chart, move the mouse ⌕ over **Finish** and then press the left mouse button.

■ The chart appears.

DELETE A CHART

1 Move the mouse ⌕ over a blank area in the chart and then press the left mouse button. Handles (■) appear around the chart.

2 Press Delete on your keyboard.

Note: To delete a chart displayed on a chart sheet, follow the steps to delete a worksheet. To delete a worksheet, refer to page 143.

> You can easily change the chart type to improve the way data is displayed in your chart.

CHANGE CHART TYPE

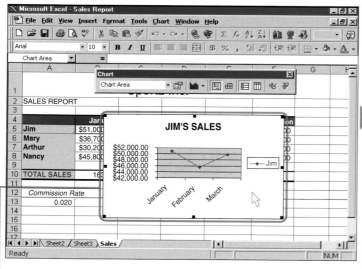

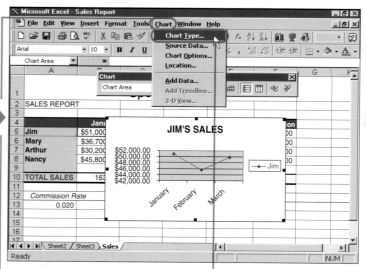

1 To change a chart on a worksheet, move the mouse ⬚ over a blank area in the chart and then press the left mouse button. Handles (■) appear around the chart.

■ To change a chart on a chart sheet, move the mouse ⬚ over the tab for the chart sheet and then press the left mouse button.

2 Move the mouse ⬚ over **Chart** and then press the left mouse button.

3 Move the mouse ⬚ over **Chart Type** and then press the left mouse button.

■ The **Chart Type** dialog box appears.

What type of chart should I choose?

The type of chart you should choose depends on your data. For example, area, column and line charts are ideal for showing changes to values over time, whereas pie charts are ideal for showing percentages.

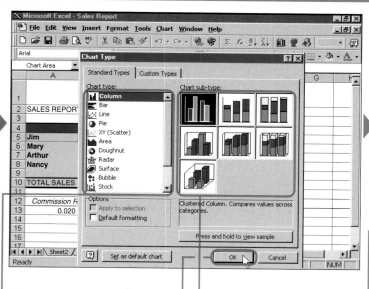

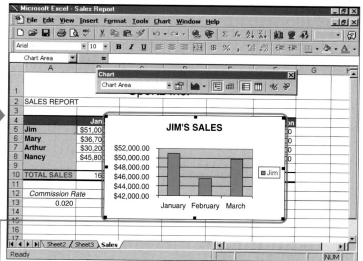

■ **4** Move the mouse ⬚ over the chart type you want to use and then press the left mouse button.

■ **5** Move the mouse ⬚ over the chart design you want to use and then press the left mouse button.

■ **6** Move the mouse ⬚ over **OK** and then press the left mouse button.

■ The chart displays the chart type you selected.

MOVE OR RESIZE A CHART

After you create a chart, you can change the location or size of the chart.

MOVE A CHART

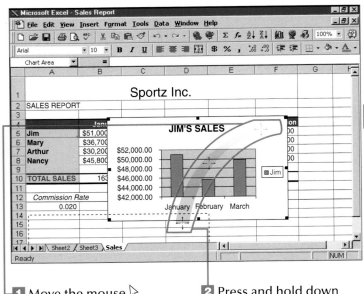

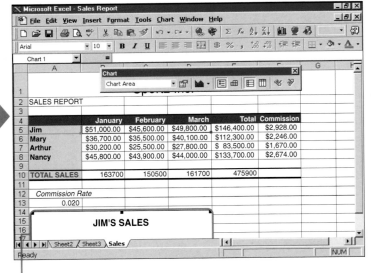

1 Move the mouse over a blank area in your chart.

2 Press and hold down the left mouse button as you move your chart to a new location.

■ A dotted line shows the new location.

3 Release the mouse button and your chart appears in the new location.

What are the handles (■) that appear around a chart?

The handles around a chart let you change the size of the chart.

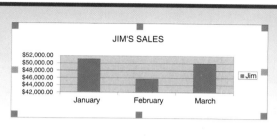

■ Change the height of a chart.

■ Change the width of a chart.

■ Change the height and width of a chart at the same time.

RESIZE A CHART

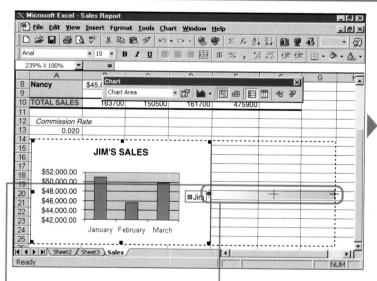

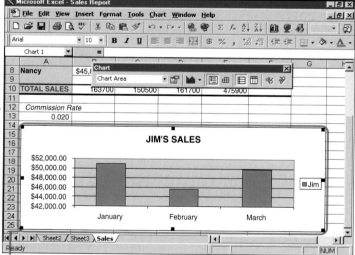

1 Move the mouse ⬉ over a blank area in your chart and then press the left mouse button. Handles (■) appear around the chart.

2 Move the mouse ⬉ over one of the handles (■) (⬉ changes to ↕ or ↔).

3 Press and hold down the left mouse button as you move the edge of your chart until the chart is the size you want.

■ A dotted line shows the new size.

4 Release the mouse button and your chart appears in the new size.

PRINT A CHART

You can print your chart with the worksheet data or on its own page.

PRINT A CHART WITH WORKSHEET DATA

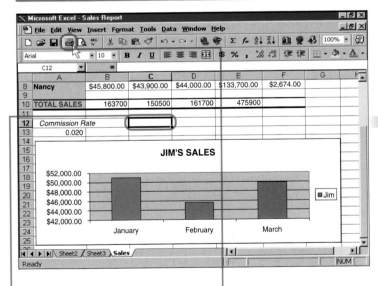

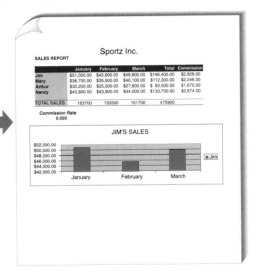

1 Move the mouse ⊹ over any cell outside your chart and then press the left mouse button.

2 Move the mouse ⇗ over 🖨 and then press the left mouse button.

Note: For more information on printing, refer to pages 120 to 137.

Can I see what my chart will look like when printed?

You can preview your chart to see what the chart will look like when printed. To preview a chart, refer to page 120.

PRINT A CHART ON ITS OWN PAGE

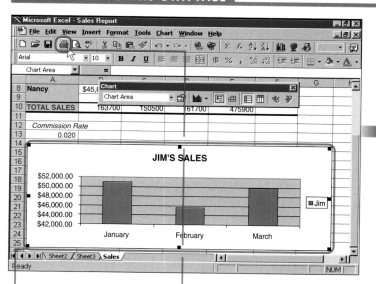

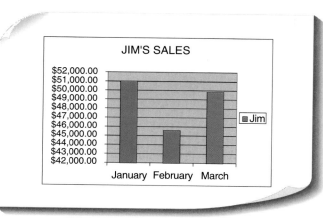

1 To print a chart displayed on a worksheet, move the mouse ⌖ over a blank area in the chart and then press the left mouse button.

■ To print a chart displayed on a chart sheet, move the mouse ⌖ over the tab for the chart sheet and then press the left mouse button.

2 Move the mouse ⌖ over 🖨 and then press the left mouse button.

Note: When you print a chart on its own page, the chart will expand to fill the page. The printed chart may look different from the chart on the worksheet.

ADD DATA TO A CHART

After you create a chart, you can easily add data to the chart.

ADD DATA TO A CHART

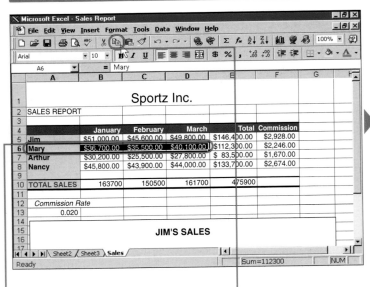

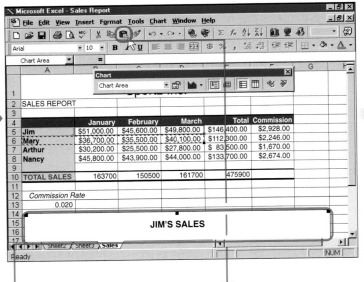

1 Select the cells containing the data you want to add to your chart, including the row or column headings. To select cells, refer to page 16.

2 To copy the data, move the mouse over 📋 and then press the left mouse button.

3 To select the chart you want to add the data to, move the mouse over the chart and then press the left mouse button.

4 To add the data to the chart, move the mouse over 📋 and then press the left mouse button.

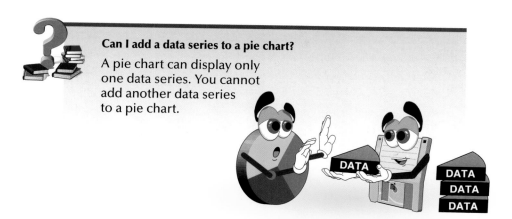

Can I add a data series to a pie chart?

A pie chart can display only one data series. You cannot add another data series to a pie chart.

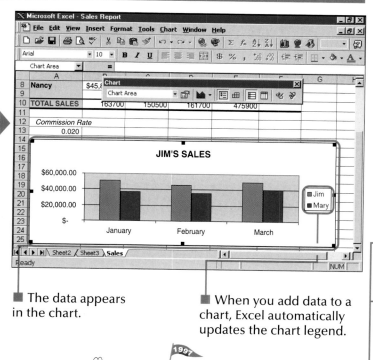

■ The data appears in the chart.

■ When you add data to a chart, Excel automatically updates the chart legend.

DELETE DATA FROM A CHART

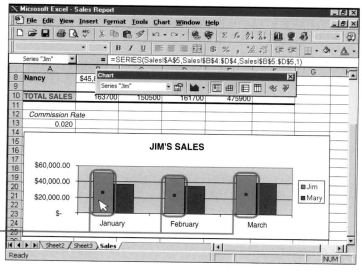

1 Move the mouse ⬚ over the data series you want to delete from your chart and then press the left mouse button.

■ Small squares (■) appear in the data series you selected.

2 To delete the data series from your chart, press `Delete` on your keyboard.

CHANGE CHART TITLES

You can change the titles in your chart to make the data more meaningful.

CHANGE CHART TITLES

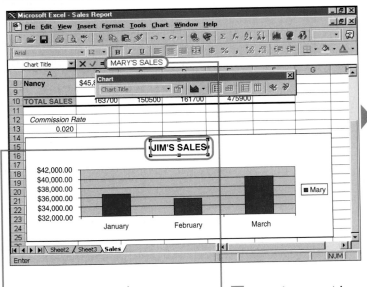

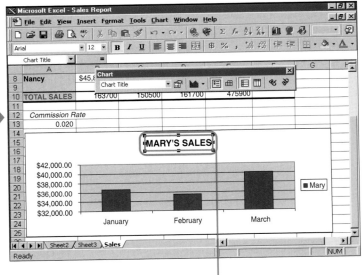

1 Move the mouse ⌖ over the title you want to change and then press the left mouse button. A border appears around the title.

2 Type the new title.

■ This area displays the text as you type.

3 Press **Enter** on your keyboard.

■ Your chart displays the new title.

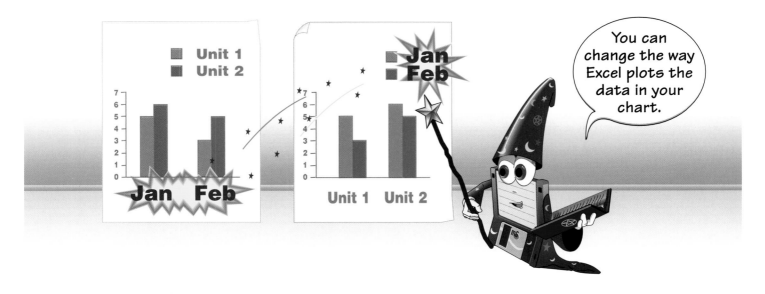

You can change the way Excel plots the data in your chart.

CHANGE THE WAY DATA IS PLOTTED

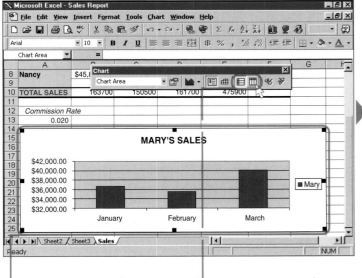

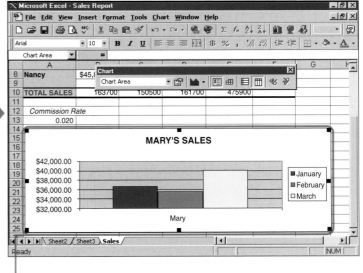

1 Move the mouse ᐅ over your chart and then press the left mouse button.

2 Move the mouse ᐅ over one of the following options and then press the left mouse button.

▤ Plot data by row

▥ Plot data by column

*Note: If ▤ and ▥ are not displayed, refer to page 82 to display the **Chart** toolbar.*

■ Your chart displays the changes.

■ To once again change the way data is plotted, repeat steps **1** and **2**.

ADD A DATA TABLE TO A CHART

You can add a table to your chart to display the data used to create the chart.

ADD A DATA TABLE TO A CHART

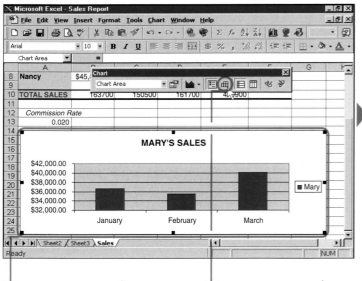

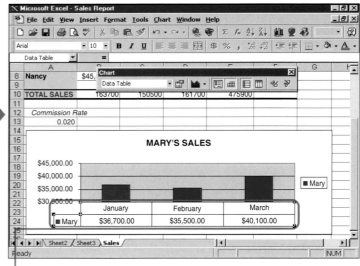

1 Move the mouse ⤢ over the chart you want to display a data table and then press the left mouse button.

Note: You cannot add a data table to some chart types.

2 Move the mouse ⤢ over ⊞ and then press the left mouse button.

Note: If ⊞ is not displayed, refer to page 82 to display the ***Chart*** *toolbar.*

■ The data table appears in the chart.

■ To hide the data table, repeat steps **1** and **2**.

168

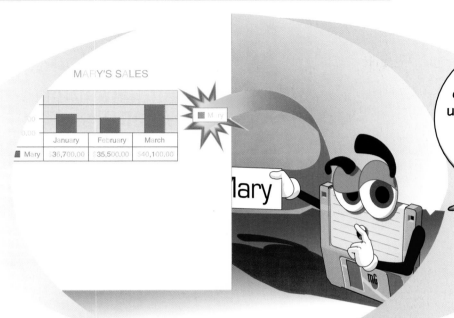

The chart legend identifies the color, pattern or symbol used for each data series in your chart. You can display or hide the chart legend at any time.

DISPLAY OR HIDE THE CHART LEGEND

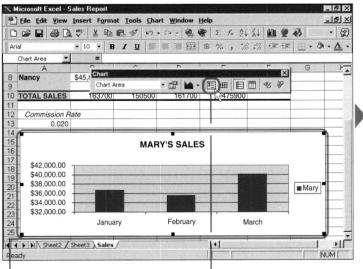

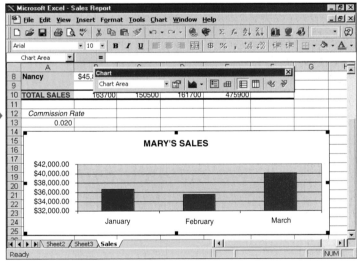

1 To display or hide the legend in a chart, move the mouse ⩗ over the chart and then press the left mouse button.

2 Move the mouse ⩗ over 🖻 and then press the left mouse button.

*Note: If 🖻 is not displayed, refer to page 82 to display the **Chart** toolbar.*

■ Excel displays or hides the chart legend.

DISPLAY DATA IN A MAP

> You can create a map to display data from your worksheet.

Excel offers maps of places around the world.

CREATE A MAP

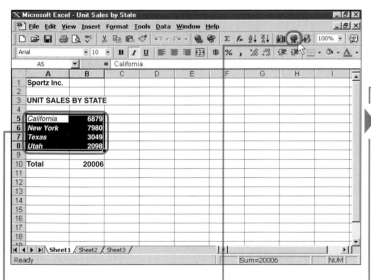

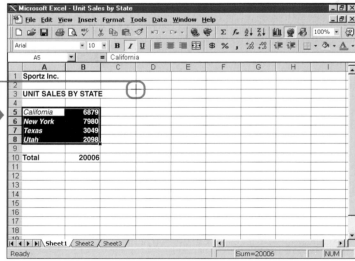

1 Select the cells containing the data you want to display in a map. To select cells, refer to page 16.

Note: One column must contain geographic data, such as country or state names.

2 Move the mouse ⌖ over 🌐 and then press the left mouse button.

■ The mouse ⌖ changes to + when over your worksheet.

3 Move the mouse + over the location where you want the top left corner of the map to appear and then press the left mouse button.

Note: If an error message appears, you need to add the Microsoft Map feature from the Microsoft Excel or Microsoft Office CD-ROM disc.

Can I move or resize a map?

You can move or resize a map as you would move or resize a chart. To move or resize a chart, refer to page 160.

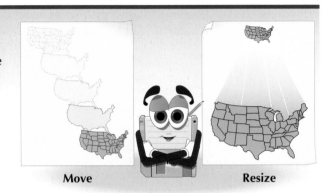

Move   **Resize**

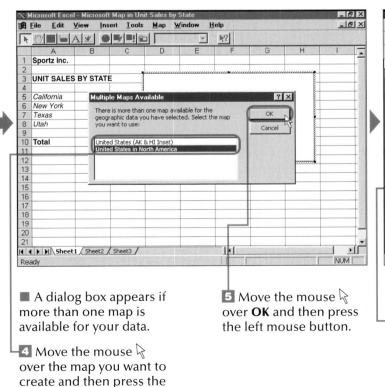

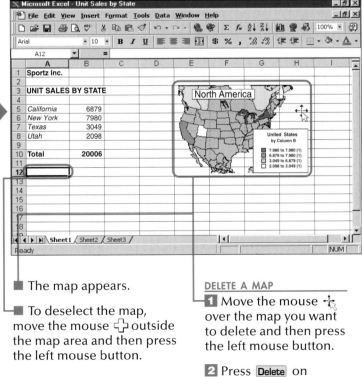

■ A dialog box appears if more than one map is available for your data.

4 Move the mouse over the map you want to create and then press the left mouse button.

5 Move the mouse over **OK** and then press the left mouse button.

■ The map appears.

■ To deselect the map, move the mouse outside the map area and then press the left mouse button.

DELETE A MAP

1 Move the mouse over the map you want to delete and then press the left mouse button.

2 Press Delete on your keyboard.

171

DISPLAY DATA IN A MAP

If you change data used in your map, you can update the map to reflect the changes.

UPDATE A MAP

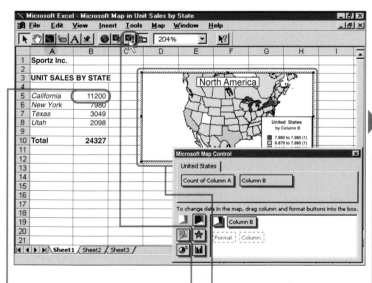

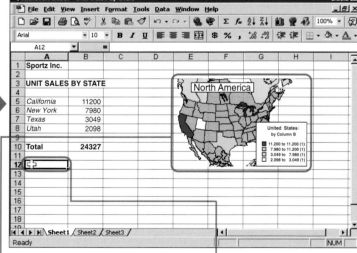

■ In this example, **6879** was changed to **11200**.

1 Move the mouse over the map you want to update and then quickly press the left mouse button twice.

2 To update the map, move the mouse over ▣! and then press the left mouse button.

■ The map updates to reflect the changes.

■ To deselect the map, move the mouse ✛ outside the map area and then press the left mouse button.

172

ADD TEXT TO A MAP

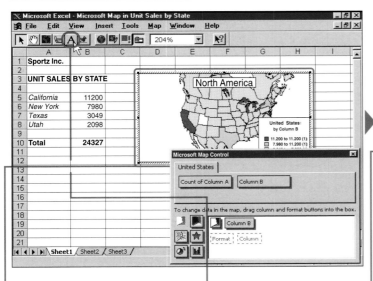

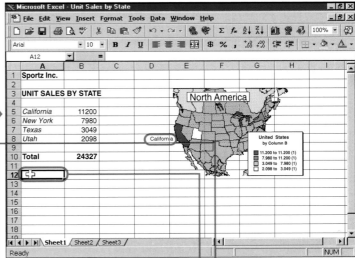

1 Move the mouse over the map you want to add text to and then quickly press the left mouse button twice.

2 To add text to the map, move the mouse over **A** and then press the left mouse button.

3 Move the mouse I over the location where you want the text to appear and then press the left mouse button.

4 Type the text and then press **Enter** on your keyboard.

■ To deselect the map, move the mouse outside the map area and then press the left mouse button.

CHAPTER 10

WORK WITH GRAPHICS

Are you wondering how to use graphics to enhance the appearance of your worksheet? This chapter shows you how.

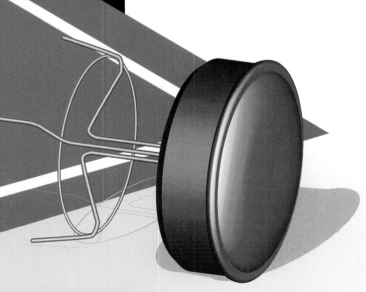

ADD A SIMPLE SHAPE

Excel provides many ready-made shapes, called AutoShapes, that you can easily add to your worksheet or chart.

ADD A SIMPLE SHAPE

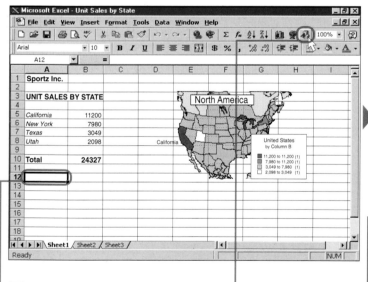

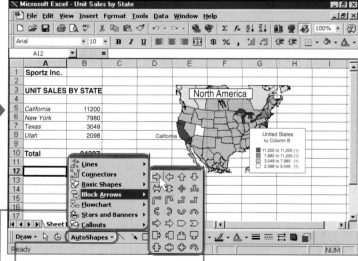

1 To add a simple shape to your worksheet, move the mouse 🕂 over any cell and then press the left mouse button.

■ To add a simple shape to your chart, move the mouse ↖ over the chart and then press the left mouse button.

2 To display the **Drawing** toolbar, move the mouse ↖ over 🖼 and then press the left mouse button.

3 To add a simple shape, move the mouse ↖ over **AutoShapes** and then press the left mouse button.

4 Move the mouse ↖ over the type of shape you want to add.

5 Move the mouse ↖ over the shape you want to add and then press the left mouse button.

Can I add text to a simple shape?

1 To add text to a simple shape, move the mouse over the shape and then press the left mouse button.

2 Type the text.

Note: You cannot add text to some simple shapes.

3 To deselect the shape, move the mouse ⊕ outside the shape area and then press the left mouse button.

CONGRATULATIONS!

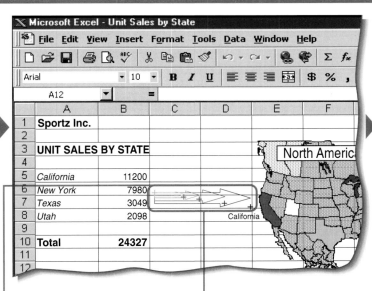

6 Move the mouse ⊳ to where you want the top left corner of the shape to appear (⊳ changes to +).

7 Press and hold down the left mouse button as you move the mouse + until the shape is the size you want. Then release the mouse button.

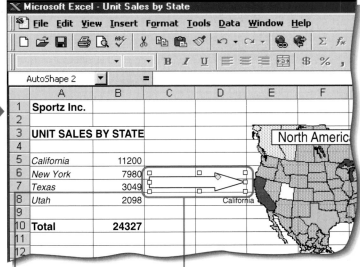

■ The shape appears. The handles (□) around the shape let you change the size of the shape. To resize a graphic, refer to page 183.

■ To hide the **Drawing** toolbar, repeat step **2**.

DELETE A SHAPE

■ Move the mouse ⊕ over an edge of the shape (⊕ changes to ⊹) and then press the left mouse button. Then press `Delete` on your keyboard.

ADD A TEXT BOX

You can add a text box to your worksheet or chart to display comments or additional information.

ADD A TEXT BOX

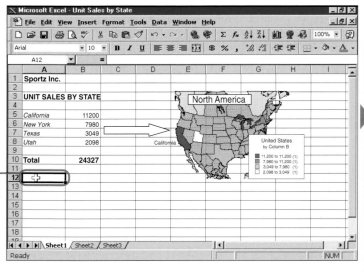

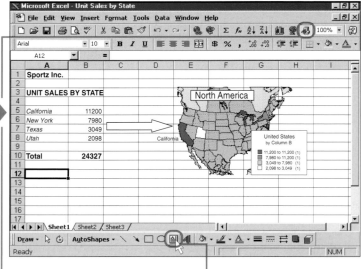

1 To add a text box to your worksheet, move the mouse ✛ over any cell and then press the left mouse button.

■ To add a text box to your chart, move the mouse ⍨ over the chart and then press the left mouse button.

2 To display the **Drawing** toolbar, move the mouse ⍨ over 🖌 and then press the left mouse button.

3 To add a text box, move the mouse ⍨ over 📰 and then press the left mouse button.

How do I delete a text box?

1 To delete a text box, move the mouse ✛ over an edge of the text box and then press the left mouse button.

2 Press Delete on your keyboard.

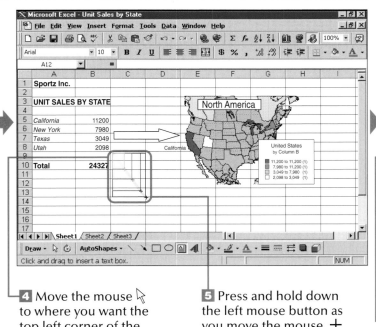

4 Move the mouse ⊢ to where you want the top left corner of the text box to appear (⊢ changes to ↓).

5 Press and hold down the left mouse button as you move the mouse **+** until the text box is the size you want. Then release the mouse button.

■ The text box appears.

6 Type the text you want to appear in the text box.

7 To deselect the text box, move the mouse ✛ outside the text box area and then press the left mouse button.

■ To hide the **Drawing** toolbar, repeat step **2**.

ADD A TEXT EFFECT

You can use the WordArt feature to add special text effects to your worksheet or chart.

ADD A TEXT EFFECT

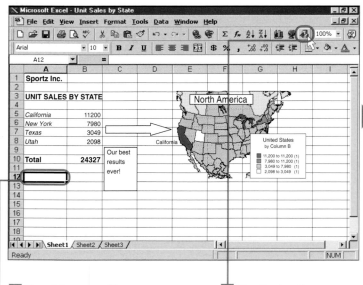

1 To add a text effect to your worksheet, move the mouse ⊕ over any cell and then press the left mouse button.

■ To add a text effect to your chart, move the mouse ↖ over the chart and then press the left mouse button.

2 To display the **Drawing** toolbar, move the mouse ↖ over 📊 and then press the left mouse button.

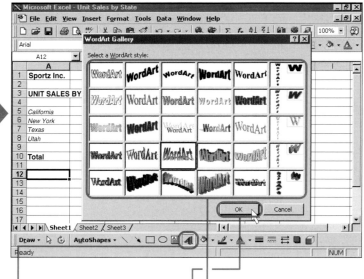

3 To add a text effect, move the mouse ↖ over 📈 and then press the left mouse button.

■ The **WordArt Gallery** dialog box appears.

4 Move the mouse ↖ over the type of text effect you want to add and then press the left mouse button.

5 Move the mouse ↖ over **OK** and then press the left mouse button.

How do I delete a text effect?

1 To delete a text effect, move the mouse 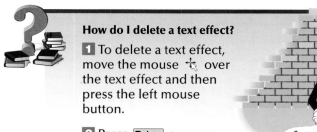 over the text effect and then press the left mouse button.

2 Press Delete on your keyboard.

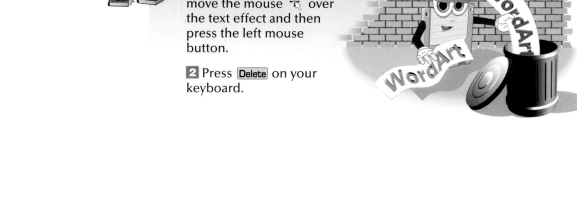

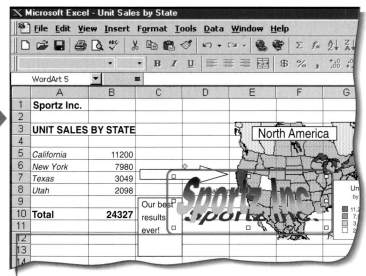

■ The **Edit WordArt Text** dialog box appears.

6 Type the text you want to display the effect you selected.

7 Move the mouse ↳ over **OK** and then press the left mouse button.

■ The text effect appears. The handles (□) around the text effect let you change the size of the effect. To resize a graphic, refer to page 183.

■ To deselect the text effect, move the mouse ⊕ outside the text effect area and then press the left mouse button.

■ To hide the **Drawing** toolbar, repeat step 2.

MOVE OR RESIZE A GRAPHIC

You can easily change the location or size of a graphic in your worksheet or chart.

- RESIZE -

- MOVE -

MOVE A GRAPHIC

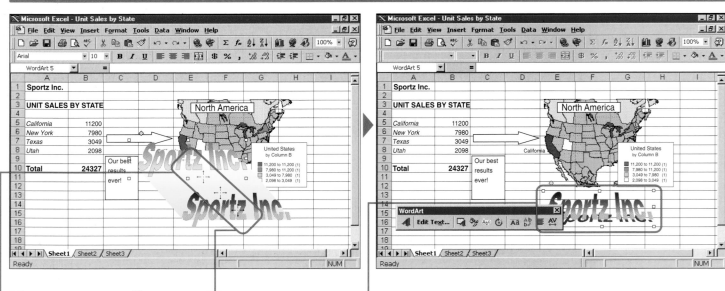

1 Move the mouse ✛ over the graphic you want to move (✛ changes to ✣).

2 Press and hold down the left mouse button as you move the graphic to a new location. Then release the mouse button.

■ The graphic appears in the new location.

Note: You cannot move a graphic you added to a chart outside of the chart area.

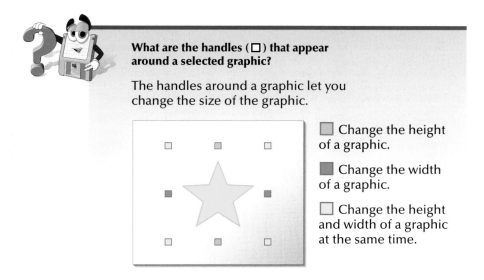

What are the handles (□) that appear around a selected graphic?

The handles around a graphic let you change the size of the graphic.

■ Change the height of a graphic.

■ Change the width of a graphic.

□ Change the height and width of a graphic at the same time.

RESIZE A GRAPHIC

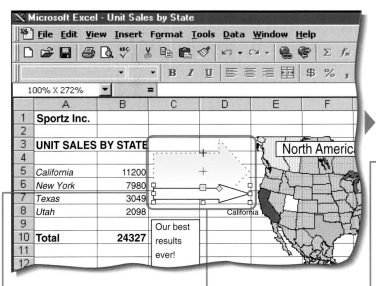

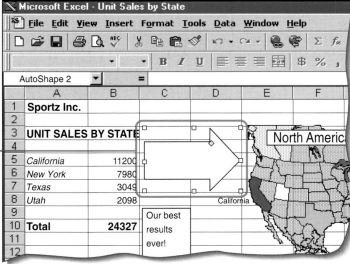

■1 Move the mouse ⊹ over the graphic you want to resize (⊹ changes to ⊹) and then press the left mouse button. Handles (□) appear around the graphic.

■2 Move the mouse ⊹ over one of the handles (⊹ changes to ↔ or ↕).

■3 Press and hold down the left mouse button as you move the mouse ✛ until the graphic is the size you want. Then release the mouse button.

■ The graphic appears in the new size.

CHANGE COLOR OF GRAPHIC

You can easily change the color of a graphic in your worksheet or chart.

CHANGE COLOR OF GRAPHIC

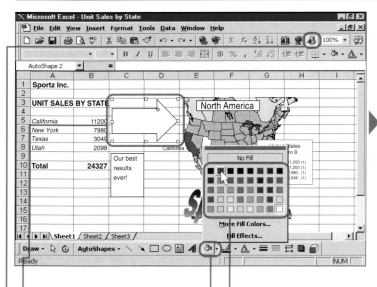

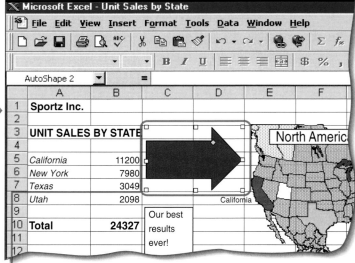

1 Move the mouse ⊕ over the graphic you want to display a different color (⊕ changes to ⬚) and then press the left mouse button.

2 To display the **Drawing** toolbar, move the mouse ⬚ over 🖌 and then press the left mouse button.

3 Move the mouse ⬚ over ▼ in this area and then press the left mouse button.

4 Move the mouse ⬚ over the color you want to use and then press the left mouse button.

■ The graphic displays the color you selected.

■ To hide the **Drawing** toolbar, repeat step **2**.

184

You can make a graphic in your worksheet or chart appear three dimensional.

MAKE A GRAPHIC 3-D

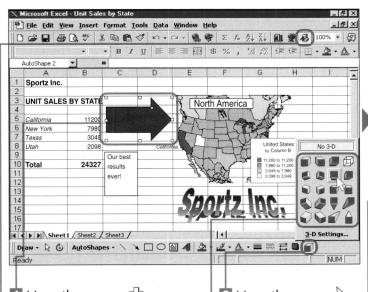

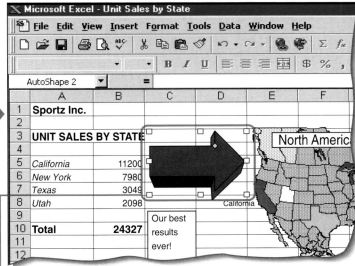

1 Move the mouse 🕂 over the graphic you want to make 3-D (🕂 changes to ⁺⃗) and then press the left mouse button.

2 To display the **Drawing** toolbar, move the mouse ⤢ over 🔲 and then press the left mouse button.

3 Move the mouse ⤢ over 🔲 and then press the left mouse button.

4 Move the mouse ⤢ over the 3-D effect you want to use and then press the left mouse button.

■ The graphic appears in 3-D.

■ To hide the **Drawing** toolbar, repeat step **2**.

CHAPTER 11

MANAGE DATA IN A LIST

Would you like Excel to help you organize and analyze a large collection of data? In this chapter you will learn how to sort data in a list, add subtotals to a list and more.

INTRODUCTION TO LISTS

Excel provides powerful tools for organizing and analyzing a large collection of data.

COMMON LISTS

Common lists include mailing lists, phone directories, product lists, library book catalogs, music collections and wine lists.

PARTS OF A LIST

Column Labels
The first row in a list contains column labels. Column labels describe the data in each column.

Records
Each row in a list contains one record. A record is a group of related data.

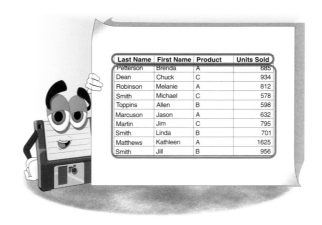

Last Name	First Name	Product	Units Sold
Petterson	Brenda	A	685
Dean	Chuck	C	934
Robinson	Melanie	A	812
Smith	Michael	C	578
Toppins	Allen	B	598
Marcuson	Jason	A	632
Martin	Jim	C	795
Smith	Linda	B	701
Matthews	Kathleen	A	1625
Smith	Jill	B	956

CREATE A LIST

You can create and store a list in a worksheet.

Record 1

Last Name **Petterson**
First Name **Brenda**
Product **A**
Units Sold **685**

CREATE A LIST

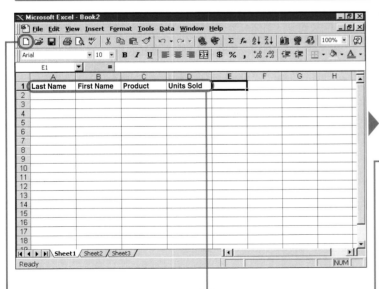

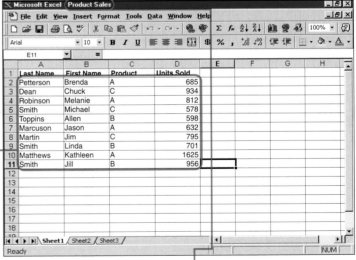

1 To create a new workbook for your list, move the mouse ⬚ over ⬚ and then press the left mouse button.

2 Type the column labels that describe the data you will enter into each column.

Note: To bold the column labels, refer to page 92. To change the width of the columns, refer to page 90.

3 Type the information for each record. Do not leave any blank rows in your list.

4 Save your workbook. To save a workbook, refer to page 24.

SORT DATA IN A LIST

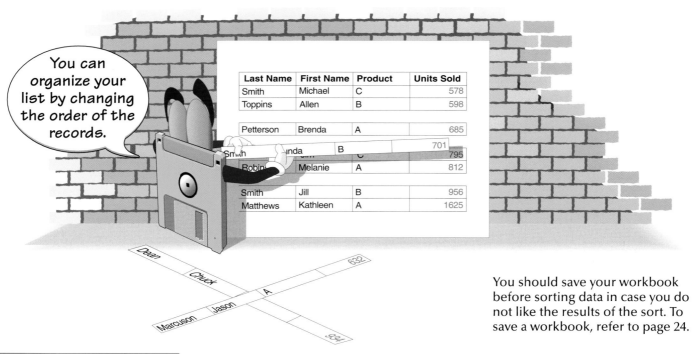

You can organize your list by changing the order of the records.

You should save your workbook before sorting data in case you do not like the results of the sort. To save a workbook, refer to page 24.

(refer to page 24.)

SORT DATA BY ONE COLUMN

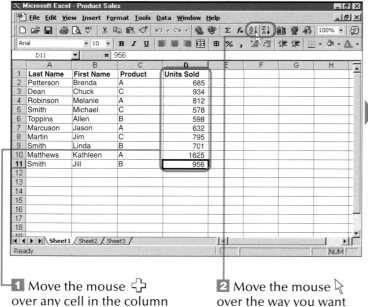

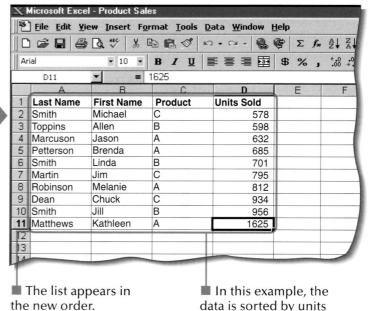

1 Move the mouse ⊕ over any cell in the column you want to sort by and then press the left mouse button.

2 Move the mouse ⟍ over the way you want to sort the data and then press the left mouse button.

▢↓ Sort 0 to 9, A to Z

▢↓ Sort 9 to 0, Z to A

■ The list appears in the new order.

■ In this example, the data is sorted by units sold.

190

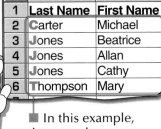

You can sort your data by more than one column.

	A	B
1	**Last Name**	**First Name**
2	Carter	Michael
3	Jones	Beatrice
4	Jones	Allan
5	Jones	Cathy
6	Thompson	Mary

	A	B
1	**Last Name**	**First Name**
2	Carter	Michael
3	Jones	Allan
4	Jones	Beatrice
5	Jones	Cathy
6	Thompson	Mary

■ In this example, the records are sorted alphabetically by last name.

■ If a last name appears more than once in your list, you can sort by a second column, such as first name.

SORT DATA BY TWO COLUMNS

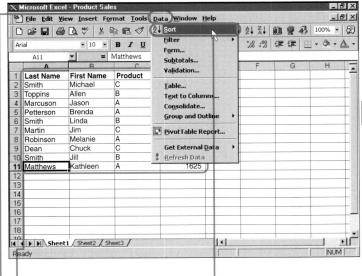

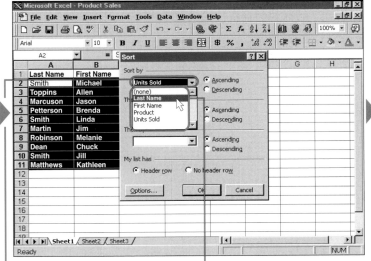

1 Move the mouse ⊕ over any cell in your list and then press the left mouse button.

2 Move the mouse ⇖ over **Data** and then press the left mouse button.

3 Move the mouse ⇖ over **Sort** and then press the left mouse button.

■ The **Sort** dialog box appears.

4 To identify the first column you want to sort by, move the mouse ⇖ over ▼ in this area and then press the left mouse button.

5 Move the mouse ⇖ over the label for the first column you want to sort by and then press the left mouse button.

CONTINUED➡

SORT DATA IN A LIST

You can sort the data in your list by letter, number or date.

LETTER	NUMBER	DATE
A	100	Jan-97
B	200	Feb-97
C	300	Mar-97
D	400	Apr-97
E	500	May-97
F	600	Jun-97
G	700	Jul-97
H	800	Aug-97

SORT DATA BY TWO COLUMNS (CONTINUED)

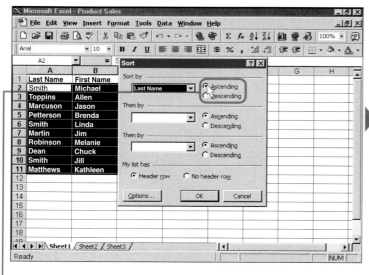

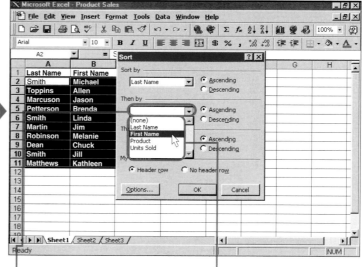

6 Move the mouse ⊳ over the way you want to sort the first column and then press the left mouse button (○ changes to ◉).

Ascending
Sort 0 to 9, A to Z

Descending
Sort 9 to 0, Z to A

7 To identify the second column you want to sort by, move the mouse ⊳ over ▼ in this area and then press the left mouse button.

8 Move the mouse ⊳ over the label for the second column you want to sort by and then press the left mouse button.

How often can I sort my list?

You can sort your list as often as you like. This is ideal if you are constantly adding new records to the list.

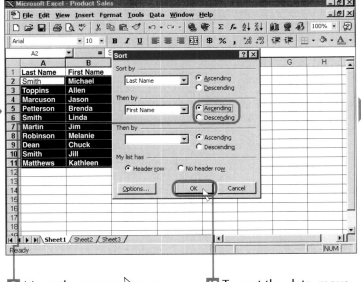

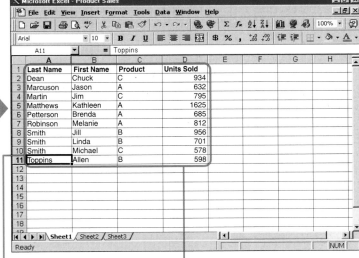

9 Move the mouse ⮕ over the way you want to sort the second column and then press the left mouse button (○ changes to ◉).

10 To sort the data, move the mouse ⮕ over **OK** and then press the left mouse button.

■ The list appears in the new order.

■ In this example, the data is sorted by last name. All records with the same last name are then sorted by first name.

FILTER DATA IN A LIST

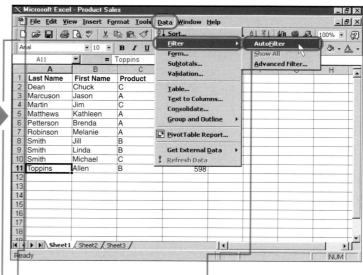

You can filter your list to display only the records containing the data you want to review.

FILTER DATA IN A LIST

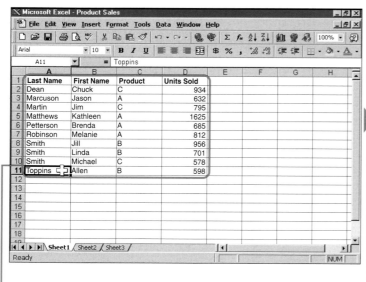

1 Move the mouse ⊕ over any cell in your list and then press the left mouse button.

2 Move the mouse ⍄ over **Data** and then press the left mouse button.

3 Move the mouse ⍄ over **Filter**.

4 Move the mouse ⍄ over **AutoFilter** and then press the left mouse button.

How does the AutoFilter feature help me analyze data?

The AutoFilter feature lets you easily analyze your data by placing related records together and hiding the records you do not want to review.

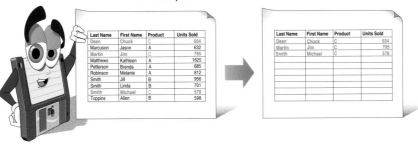

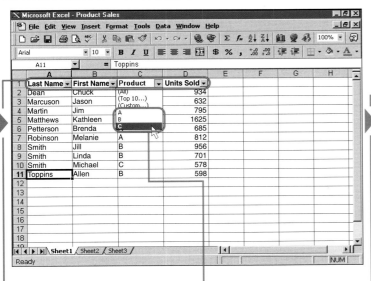

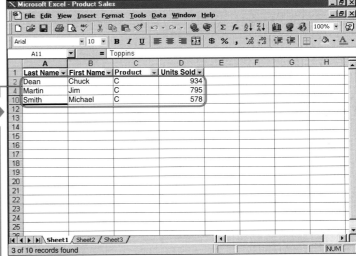

■ An arrow (▾) appears beside each column label.

5 Move the mouse ⏳ over ▾ in the column containing the data you want to use to filter the list and then press the left mouse button.

6 Move the mouse ⏳ over the data you want to use to filter the list and then press the left mouse button.

■ The list displays only the records containing the data you specified. The other records are temporarily hidden.

■ In this example, the list displays only the records containing product C.

■ To turn off the AutoFilter feature and redisplay the entire list, repeat steps 2 to 4.

195

FILTER DATA IN A LIST

You can filter your list to display only records containing data within a specific range.

FILTER DATA—BY COMPARING VALUES

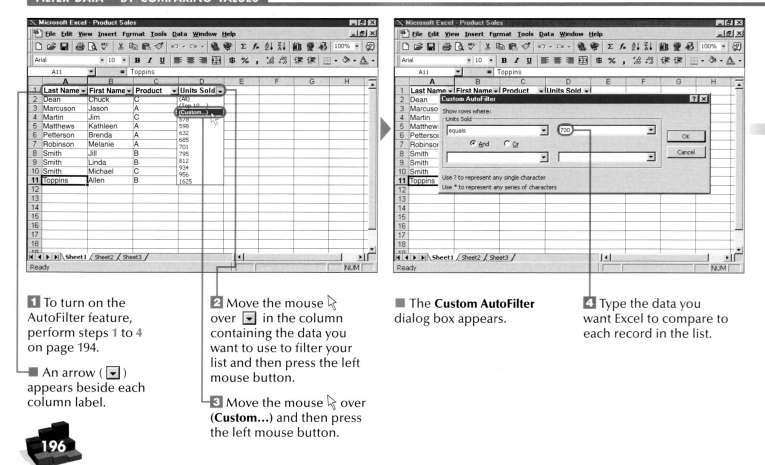

1 To turn on the AutoFilter feature, perform steps **1** to **4** on page 194.

■ An arrow (▾) appears beside each column label.

2 Move the mouse over ▾ in the column containing the data you want to use to filter your list and then press the left mouse button.

3 Move the mouse over (**Custom...**) and then press the left mouse button.

■ The **Custom AutoFilter** dialog box appears.

4 Type the data you want Excel to compare to each record in the list.

How can I compare data in my list?

Excel offers many ways you can compare data to help you analyze the information in your list.

equals
does not equal
is greater than
is greater than or equal to
is less than
is less than or equal to
begins with
does not begin with
ends with
does not end with
contains
does not contain

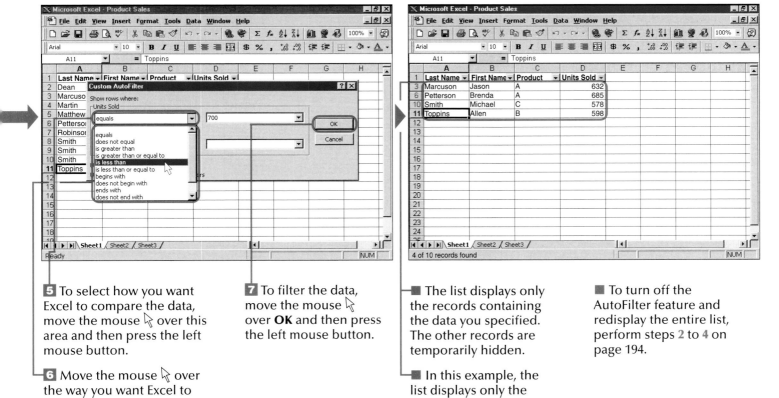

5 To select how you want Excel to compare the data, move the mouse ⬚ over this area and then press the left mouse button.

6 Move the mouse ⬚ over the way you want Excel to compare the data and then press the left mouse button.

7 To filter the data, move the mouse ⬚ over **OK** and then press the left mouse button.

■ The list displays only the records containing the data you specified. The other records are temporarily hidden.

■ In this example, the list displays only the records containing less than 700 units sold.

■ To turn off the AutoFilter feature and redisplay the entire list, perform steps 2 to 4 on page 194.

ADD SUBTOTALS TO A LIST

You can quickly summarize data by adding subtotals to your list.

ADD SUBTOTALS TO A LIST

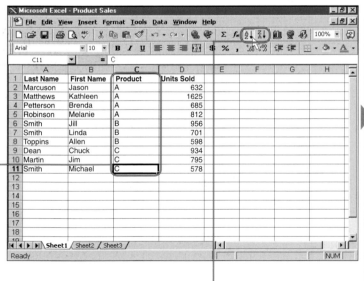

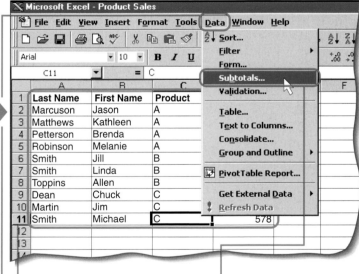

1 To sort the column you want to display subtotals for, move the mouse ⊕ over any cell in the column and then press the left mouse button.

2 Move the mouse ⊷ over the way you want to sort the data and then press the left mouse button.

A↓	Sort 0 to 9, A to Z
Z↓	Sort 9 to 0, Z to A

3 Move the mouse ⊕ over any cell in your list and then press the left mouse button.

4 Move the mouse ⊷ over **Data** and then press the left mouse button.

5 Move the mouse ⊷ over **Subtotals** and then press the left mouse button.

198

How can subtotals help me?

You can use subtotals to help you analyze the data in your list and quickly create reports and charts to summarize the data.

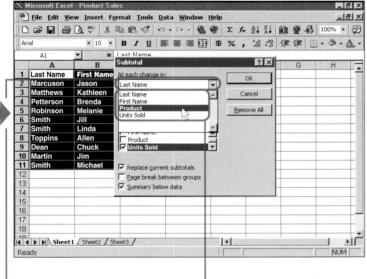

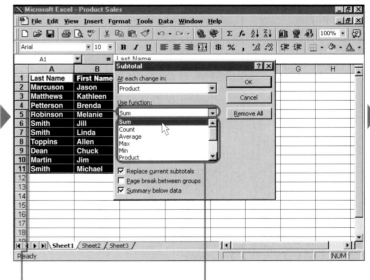

■ The **Subtotal** dialog box appears.

6 To identify the column you want to display subtotals for, move the mouse ⇱ over this area and then press the left mouse button.

7 Move the mouse ⇱ over the label of the column and then press the left mouse button.

Note: The column you identify should be the same column you sorted in step 1.

8 To select the calculation you want to perform, move the mouse ⇱ over this area and then press the left mouse button.

9 Move the mouse ⇱ over the calculation and then press the left mouse button.

CONTINUED

ADD SUBTOTALS TO A LIST

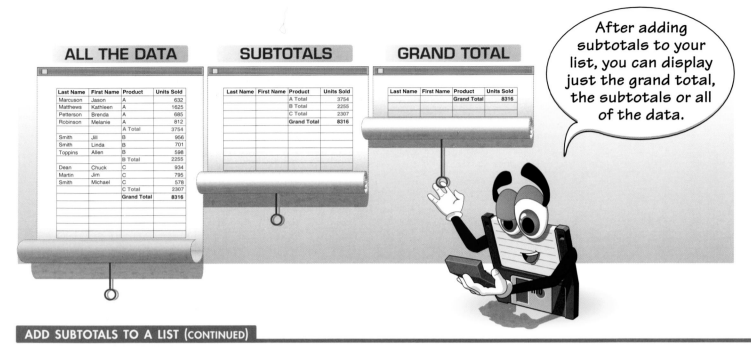

ALL THE DATA

Last Name	First Name	Product	Units Sold
Marcuson	Jason	A	632
Matthews	Kathleen	A	1625
Petterson	Brenda	A	685
Robinson	Melanie	A	812
		A Total	3754
Smith	Jill	B	956
Smith	Linda	B	701
Toppins	Allen	B	598
		B Total	2255
Dean	Chuck	C	934
Martin	Jim	C	795
Smith	Michael	C	578
		C Total	2307
		Grand Total	8316

SUBTOTALS

Last Name	First Name	Product	Units Sold
		A Total	3754
		B Total	2255
		C Total	2307
		Grand Total	8316

GRAND TOTAL

Last Name	First Name	Product	Units Sold
		Grand Total	8316

> After adding subtotals to your list, you can display just the grand total, the subtotals or all of the data.

ADD SUBTOTALS TO A LIST (CONTINUED)

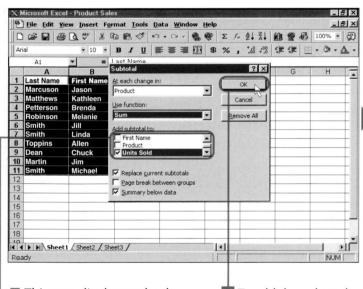

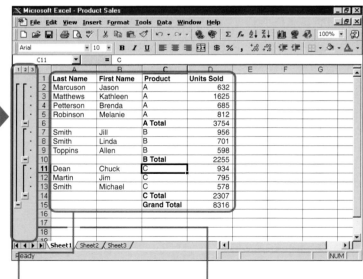

■ This area displays a check mark (✔) beside the column that Excel will subtotal.

10 To add or remove a check mark, move the mouse ⟋ over the box beside the column and then press the left mouse button.

11 To add the subtotals to your list, move the mouse ⟋ over **OK** and then press the left mouse button.

■ The list displays the subtotals and a grand total.

■ These symbols help you work with the data.

200

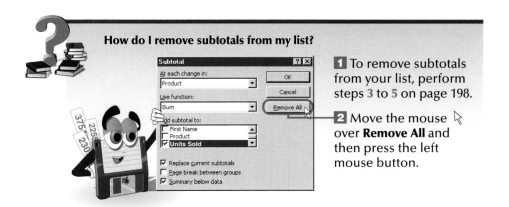

How do I remove subtotals from my list?

1 To remove subtotals from your list, perform steps 3 to 5 on page 198.

2 Move the mouse over **Remove All** and then press the left mouse button.

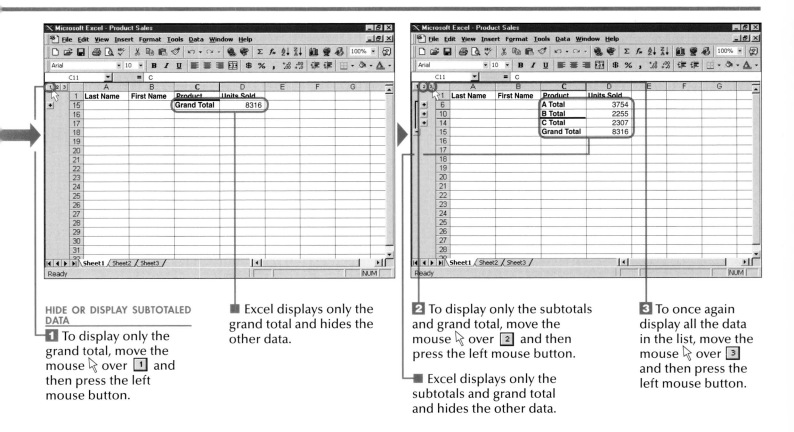

HIDE OR DISPLAY SUBTOTALED DATA

1 To display only the grand total, move the mouse over **1** and then press the left mouse button.

■ Excel displays only the grand total and hides the other data.

2 To display only the subtotals and grand total, move the mouse over **2** and then press the left mouse button.

■ Excel displays only the subtotals and grand total and hides the other data.

3 To once again display all the data in the list, move the mouse over **3** and then press the left mouse button.

CHAPTER 12

EXCEL AND THE INTERNET

Do you want to make your worksheet available on your company's intranet or the Web? Find out how in this chapter.

CREATE A HYPERLINK

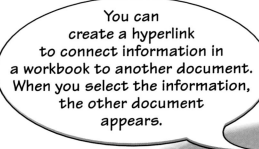

You can create a hyperlink to connect information in a workbook to another document. When you select the information, the other document appears.

CREATE A HYPERLINK

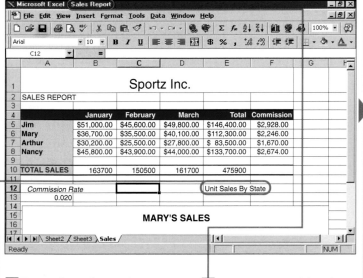

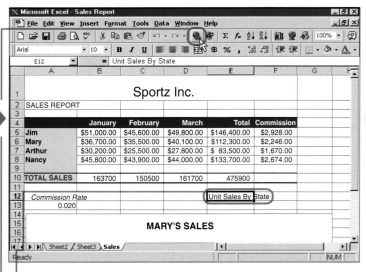

1 Enter the information you want to link to another document.

2 Save your workbook. To save a workbook, refer to page 24.

3 Select the cell(s) containing the information you entered in step 1. To select cells, refer to page 16.

4 Move the mouse ⌖ over 🔲 and then press the left mouse button.

■ The **Insert Hyperlink** dialog box appears.

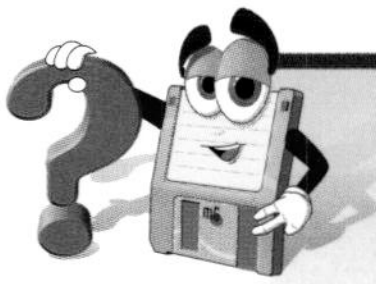

Where can a hyperlink take me?

You can create a hyperlink that takes you to another document on your computer, network, corporate intranet or the Internet.

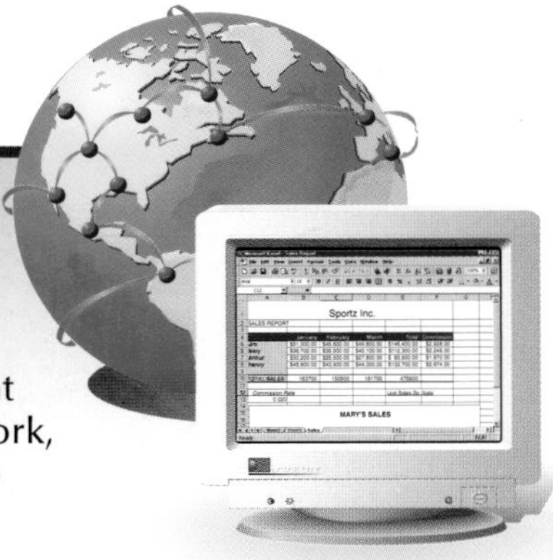

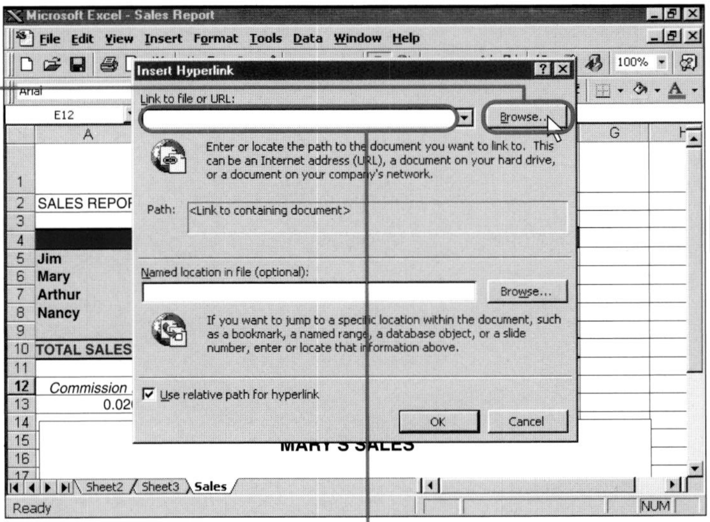

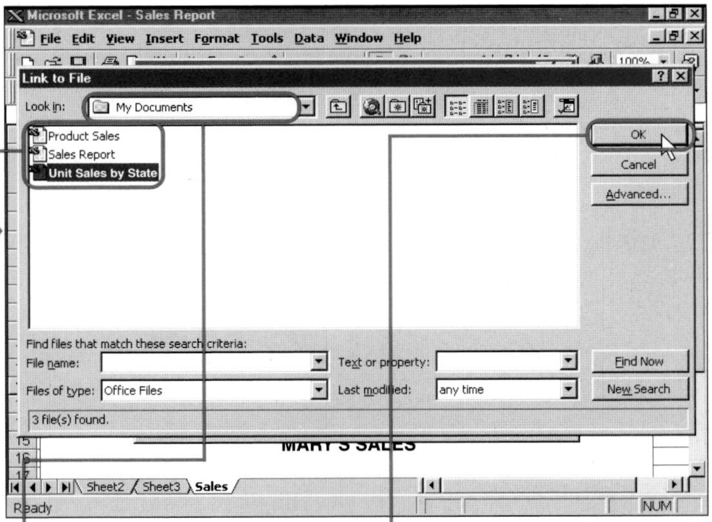

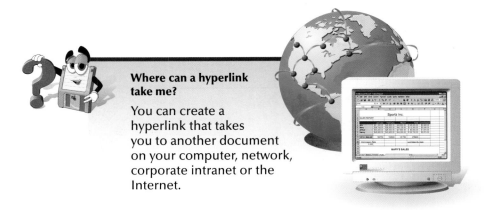

5 To link the information to a document on your computer or network, move the mouse over **Browse** and then press the left mouse button.

■ To link the information to a Web page, type the address of the Web page (example: http://www.maran.com). Then skip to step **8** on page 206.

■ The **Link to File** dialog box appears.

■ This area indicates where the documents listed in the dialog box are located.

6 Move the mouse over the document you want the information to link to and then press the left mouse button.

7 Move the mouse over **OK** and then press the left mouse button.

CONTINUED

CREATE A HYPERLINK

You can easily see hyperlinks in your workbook. Hyperlinks appear underlined and in color.

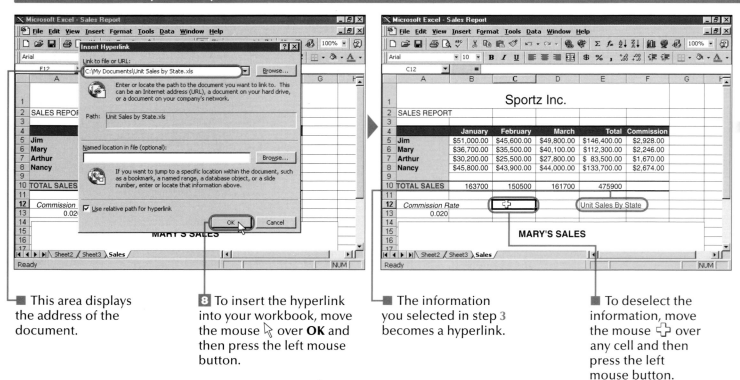

■ This area displays the address of the document.

8 To insert the hyperlink into your workbook, move the mouse ⩗ over **OK** and then press the left mouse button.

■ The information you selected in step **3** becomes a hyperlink.

■ To deselect the information, move the mouse ⨁ over any cell and then press the left mouse button.

What information can I use as a hyperlink?

You can use any information in a workbook as a hyperlink, including worksheet data, charts and maps. Make sure the information you choose clearly indicates where the hyperlink will take you. Avoid the phrase "click here" since this is not very informative.

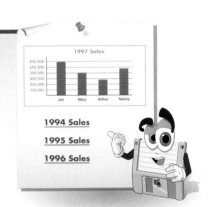

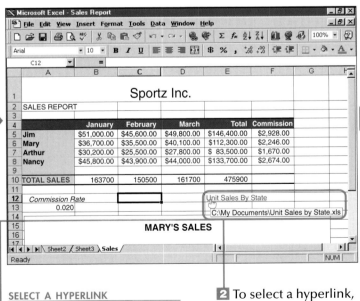

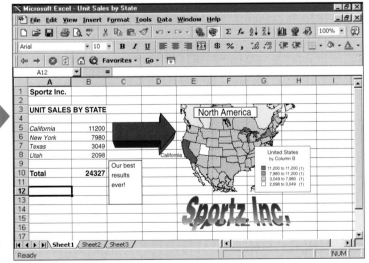

SELECT A HYPERLINK

1 To display the destination address of a hyperlink, move the mouse ⊹ over the hyperlink (⊹ changes to 🖑). After a few seconds, the address appears.

2 To select a hyperlink, move the mouse ⊹ over the hyperlink (⊹ changes to 🖑) and then press the left mouse button.

■ The document connected to the hyperlink appears.

■ If the hyperlink is connected to a Web page, your Web browser opens and displays the Web page.

DISPLAY THE WEB TOOLBAR

You can display the Web toolbar to help you browse through documents containing hyperlinks.

DISPLAY THE WEB TOOLBAR

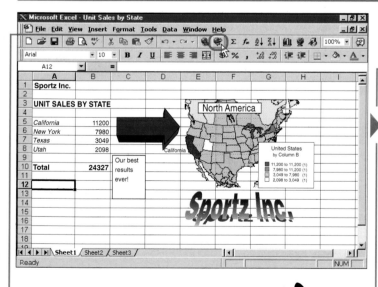

1 To display the **Web** toolbar, move the mouse ⌖ over 🌐 and then press the left mouse button.

■ The **Web** toolbar appears.

■ To hide the **Web** toolbar, repeat step **1**.

You can easily move back and forth between documents you have viewed by following hyperlinks.

MOVE BETWEEN DOCUMENTS

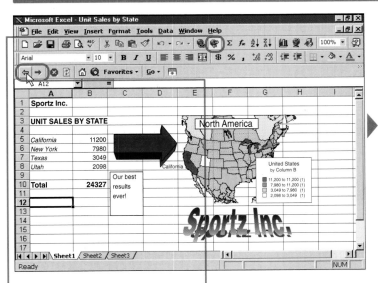

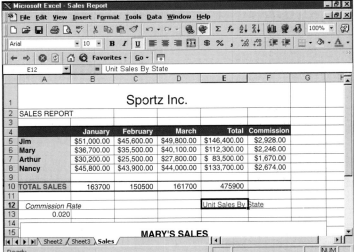

1 To display the **Web** toolbar, move the mouse ⌖ over 🌐 and then press the left mouse button.

2 Move the mouse ⌖ over one of the following options and then press the left mouse button.

⬅ Move back

➡ Move forward

■ The document you selected appears.

■ To hide the **Web** toolbar, repeat step **1**.

OPEN A DOCUMENT

You can quickly open a document that is on your computer, network, corporate intranet or the Internet.

OPEN A DOCUMENT

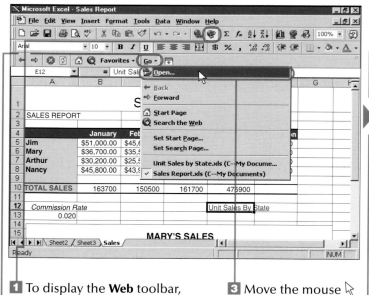

1 To display the **Web** toolbar, move the mouse ⬚ over 🔲 and then press the left mouse button.

2 To open a document, move the mouse ⬚ over **Go** and then press the left mouse button.

3 Move the mouse ⬚ over **Open** and then press the left mouse button.

■ The **Open Internet Address** dialog box appears.

4 Type the address of the document you want to open.

5 Move the mouse ⬚ over **OK** and then press the left mouse button.

If a Web page is taking a long time to appear, you can stop the transfer of information.

STOP THE CONNECTION

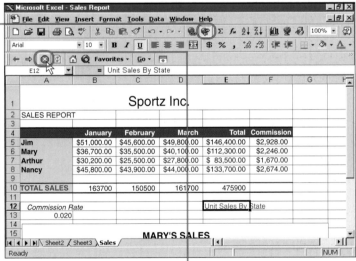

■ The document appears.

■ If you typed a Web page address in step **4**, your Web browser opens and displays the Web page.

1 To display the **Web** toolbar, move the mouse ☐ over ☐ and then press the left mouse button.

■ The **Stop** button is red (☐) when information is transferring to your computer.

2 To stop the transfer of information, move the mouse ☐ over ☐ and then press the left mouse button (☐ changes to ☐).

DISPLAY THE START PAGE

The start page is the first page that appears when you start your Web browser.

The start page includes instructions and hyperlinks that let you quickly connect to interesting documents.

DISPLAY THE START PAGE

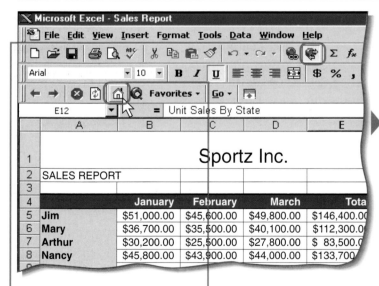

1 To display the **Web** toolbar, move the mouse ⬚ over 🌐 and then press the left mouse button.

2 To display the start page, move the mouse ⬚ over 🏠 and then press the left mouse button.

■ Your Web browser opens and displays the start page.

■ This page is automatically set as your start page.

212

The search page helps you find information of interest.

DISPLAY THE SEARCH PAGE

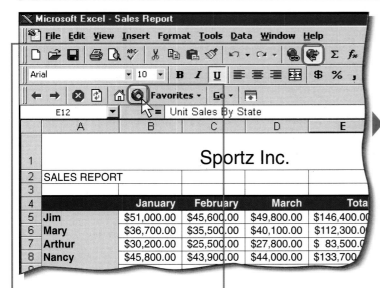

1 To display the **Web** toolbar, move the mouse over and then press the left mouse button.

2 To display the search page, move the mouse over and then press the left mouse button.

■ Your Web browser opens and displays the search page.

■ This page is automatically set as your search page.

ADD WORKBOOK TO FAVORITES

You can add workbooks you frequently use to the Favorites folder. This lets you quickly open these workbooks at any time.

ADD WORKBOOK TO FAVORITES

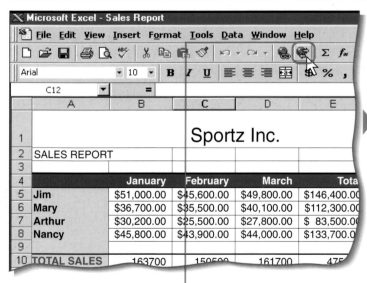

1 Open the workbook you want to add to the Favorites folder. To open a workbook, refer to page 32.

2 To display the **Web** toolbar, move the mouse ⟲ over 🌐 and then press the left mouse button.

3 Move the mouse ⟲ over **Favorites** and then press the left mouse button.

4 Move the mouse ⟲ over **Add to Favorites** and then press the left mouse button.

When I add a workbook to the Favorites folder, does the workbook change locations on my computer?

When you add a workbook to the Favorites folder, you create a shortcut to the original workbook. The original workbook does not change locations on your computer.

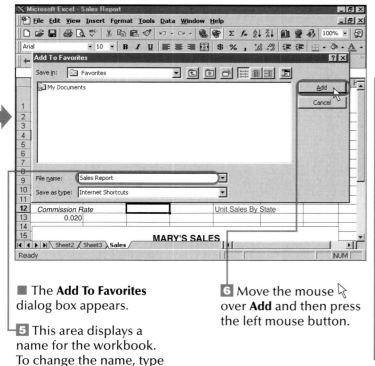

OPEN WORKBOOK IN FAVORITES

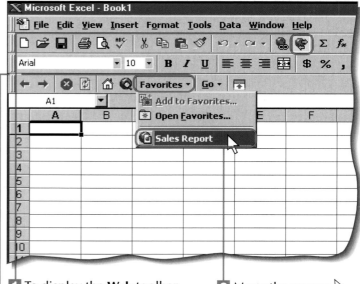

■ The **Add To Favorites** dialog box appears.

5 This area displays a name for the workbook. To change the name, type a new name.

6 Move the mouse ⌖ over **Add** and then press the left mouse button.

1 To display the **Web** toolbar, move the mouse ⌖ over 🌐 and then press the left mouse button.

2 Move the mouse ⌖ over **Favorites** and then press the left mouse button.

3 Move the mouse ⌖ over the name of the workbook you want to open and then press the left mouse button.

You can create a Web page from your worksheet data or chart. This lets you place the information on your company's intranet or the Web.

SAVE INFORMATION AS A WEB PAGE

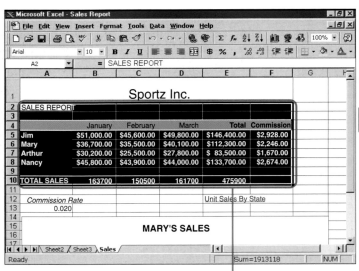

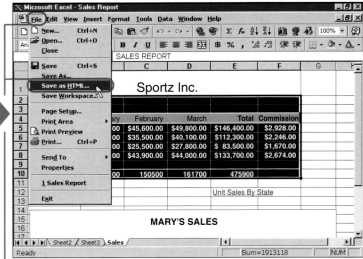

1 Open the workbook containing the information you want to save as a Web page. To open a workbook, refer to page 32.

2 Select the cells containing the information. To select cells, refer to page 16.

3 Move the mouse ⇗ over **File** and then press the left mouse button.

4 Move the mouse ⇗ over **Save as HTML** and then press the left mouse button.

*Note: If the **Save as HTML** command is not available, you need to add the Web Page Authoring (HTML) component from the Microsoft Excel or Microsoft Office CD-ROM disc.*

■ The **Internet Assistant Wizard** dialog box appears.

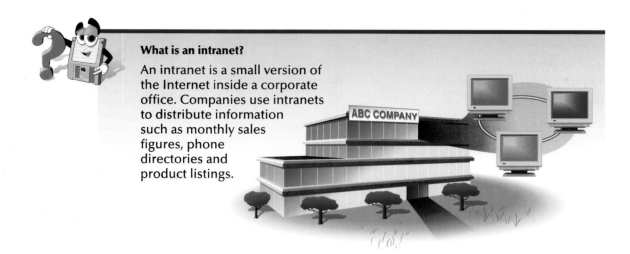

What is an intranet?

An intranet is a small version of the Internet inside a corporate office. Companies use intranets to distribute information such as monthly sales figures, phone directories and product listings.

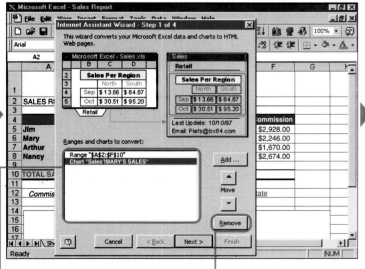

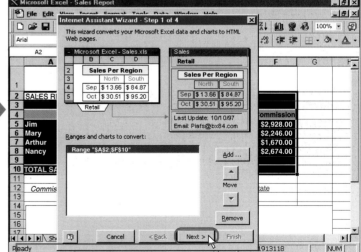

■ This area displays the cells you selected and every chart in your workbook.

5 If you do not want to include a chart on your Web page, move the mouse ⇧ over the chart and then press the left mouse button.

6 To remove the chart from the list, move the mouse ⇧ over **Remove** and then press the left mouse button.

7 To continue, move the mouse ⇧ over **Next** and then press the left mouse button.

CONTINUED➡

SAVE INFORMATION AS A WEB PAGE

Excel lets you add header and footer information to your Web page.

SAVE INFORMATION AS A WEB PAGE (CONTINUED)

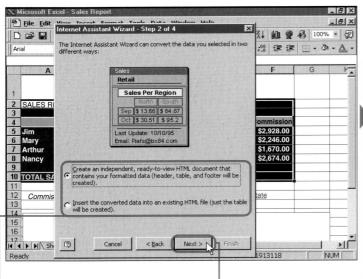

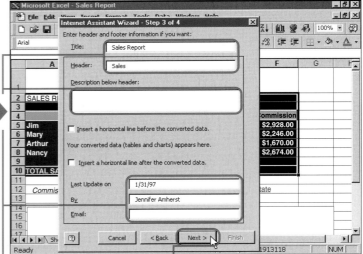

■ Excel asks if you want to create a new Web page or add the information to an existing Web page.

8 Move the mouse ⬚ over the option you want to use and then press the left mouse button (○ changes to ●).

9 To continue, move the mouse ⬚ over **Next** and then press the left mouse button.

■ The information in these areas will appear on your Web page.

10 To enter information into an area, move the mouse I over the area and then press the left mouse button. Then type the information.

Note: If an area contains information you want to delete, move the mouse I over the area and then press the left mouse button. Then press ◆Backspace or Delete on your keyboard to remove the information.

11 To continue, move the mouse ⬚ over **Next** and then press the left mouse button.

218

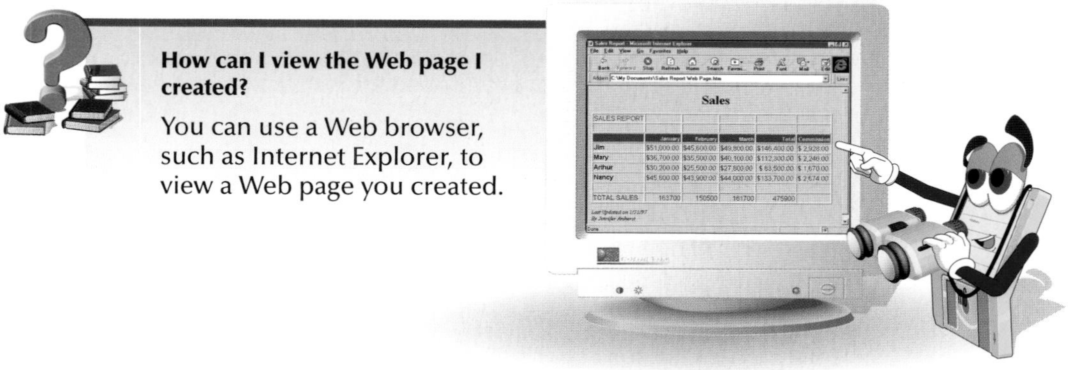

How can I view the Web page I created?

You can use a Web browser, such as Internet Explorer, to view a Web page you created.

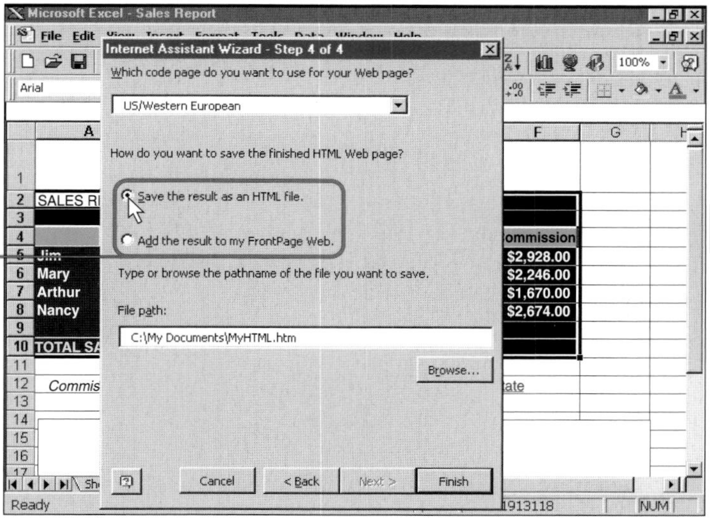

12 Move the mouse over the way you want to save the Web page and then press the left mouse button (○ changes to ◉).

Note: If you do not have FrontPage, save the result as an HTML file.

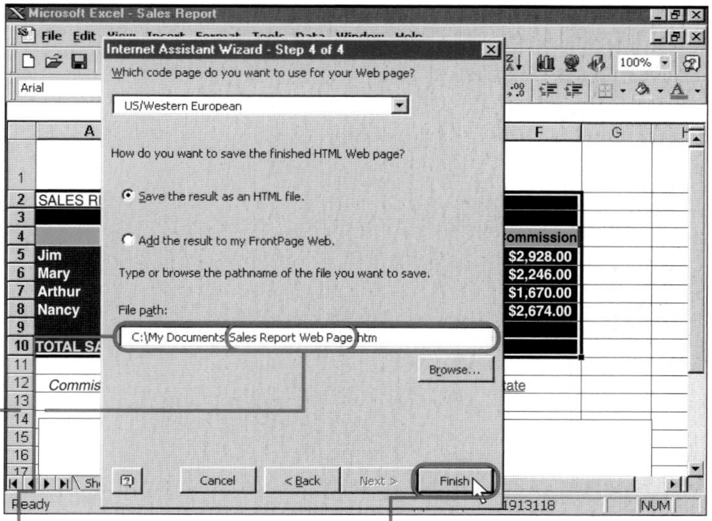

■ This area displays the location and name of the Web page.

13 To change the name of the Web page, move the mouse I over the name and then quickly press the left mouse button twice. Then type a new name.

14 To create the Web page, move the mouse over **Finish** and then press the left mouse button.

INDEX

INDEX